LETTERS TO
Sala

LETTERS TO
Sala

A Young Woman's Life in Nazi Labor Camps

Ann Kirschner

With an Essay by Debórah Dwork and Robert Jan van Pelt

THE NEW YORK PUBLIC LIBRARY
NEW YORK
2006

Published for the exhibition *Letters to Sala:
A Young Woman's Life in Nazi Labor Camps*
Curated by Jill Vexler
Presented at The New York Public Library
Humanities and Social Sciences Library
Sue and Edgar Wachenheim III Gallery
March 7–June 17, 2006

Support for this exhibition has been provided
by the Righteous Persons Foundation and
the Conference on Jewish Material Claims
Against Germany.

Support for The New York Public Library's
Exhibitions Program has been provided
by Pinewood Foundation and by Sue and
Edgar Wachenheim III.

Except where otherwise indicated, illustrations
have been drawn from the Sala Garncarz
Collection in the Dorot Jewish Division,
Humanities and Social Sciences Library,
The New York Public Library.

Library of Congress Cataloging-in-Publication
Data

Kirschner, Ann.
  Letters to Sala : a young woman's life in Nazi
labor camps / Ann Kirschner ; with an essay
by Debórah Dwork and Robert Jan van Pelt.
    p. cm.
  Published for the exhibition curated by Jill
Vexler and presented at The New York Public
Library Humanities and Social Sciences Library,
Sue and Edgar Wachenheim III Gallery, March
7–June 17, 2006.
  ISBN 0-87104-457-9 (alk. paper)
  1. Kirschner, Sala Garncarz, 1924–.
2. Kirschner, Sala Garncarz, 1924– —Corre-
spondence—Exhibitions. 3. Jews—Persecu-
tions—Poland—Sosnowiec (Województwo
Slaskie)—Biography—Exhibitions. 4. Holocaust,
Jewish (1939–1945)—Poland—Sosnowiec
(Województwo Slaskie)—Personal narra-
tives—Exhibitions. 5. Jewish children in the
Holocaust—Poland—Sosnowiec (Województwo
Slaskie)—Biography—Exhibitions. 6. World
War, 1939–1945—Conscript labor—Poland—
Exhibitions. 7. Sosnowiec (Województwo
Slaskie, Poland)—Biography—Exhibitions. 8.
Sue and Edgar Wachenheim III Gallery—Ex-
hibitions. I. Dwork, Debórah. II. Pelt, R. J. van
(Robert Jan), 1955–. III. Vexler, Jill. IV. Sue and
Edgar Wachenheim III Gallery. V. Title.
  DS135.P63K5575 2006
  940.53'18092—dc22

                                    2006001304

Printed on acid-free paper
Printed in the United States of America at
The Stinehour Press, Lunenburg, VT

Karen Van Westering, Director,
NYPL Publications
Barbara Bergeron, Editor

Designed by Kara Van Woerden

Map on page 50 created by Matthew A. Knutzen,
Assistant Chief, The Lionel Pincus and Princess
Firyal Map Division

The New York Public Library
www.nypl.org

Postkarte

Sala Garncarz Kirschner, 2005.
(Courtesy of Ann Kirschner and family)

Preface

MY MOTHER, SALA, HAD A SECRET.

Like an iceberg, only the peak was visible. She was born in Poland, and she had survived a Nazi camp. But I knew no more about her life during the war than that. It was as if she had been snatched by extraterrestrials. Where had she been during those years? When she talked about the past, she began with June 1946 when she arrived in New York as the war bride of an American soldier. I liked this story, especially since my brothers and I had starring roles. But even as a child, I could see the jagged edges of her tale. Whole chapters were missing. So fast, so complete a transformation from Sala, the survivor, to Sala, the happy American housewife and mother, seemed impossible.

Where did the old Sala go? I had no one to ask. I never discussed my mother's silence with my brothers or my father. The prohibition seemed to extend to the whole subject, even when she wasn't present. When someone else—a new friend, a careless relative—wandered into the forbidden territory of her years during the war, she turned her face away as if she had been slapped. I had a few friends in my Queens, New York, neighborhood who were also children of survivors, some with numbers on their arms, but they had no answers and they did not share my preoccupation with concentration camps; their parents wouldn't *stop* talking about the past. Enough already, my friends would say, we're tired of playing Anne Frank.

Compared to those survivors who spread a layer of the Holocaust so thickly over their children's lives that they felt doomed—or simply bored, like my old friends in Queens—Sala worked hard to protect her children from the contagion of fear. Nor did she want anyone's pity, ours least of all. Our mother was beautiful and glamorous and fun-loving. She never compared our lives to hers, never begrudged our access to education, our freedom, our middle-class amenities. Piano lessons, Boy Scouts, the beach at Rockaway, and a summer bungalow in the Catskill Mountains—she wanted us to enjoy it all.

Of course, despite her best efforts, Sala could never build an impermeable wall between our present and her past. The fog seeped in. During the televised Eichmann trial, she sat and watched for hours, chain-smoking, stony and silent. She read every Holocaust book, watched every Holocaust movie, observed every Holocaust anniversary, but she tried to encounter history covertly—as if I wasn't watching.

All that ended in 1991 on a day that would change her forever in my eyes, a day that was to change my life as well.

Sala was about to be admitted into the hospital for triple bypass surgery, and she had come to spend the weekend with my family. She was sixty-seven years old, miserable in her first week of giving up smoking, and her hands looked empty without her usual cigarette. I could tell that she was getting ready to say goodbye. It was a beautiful summer day, we had just finished lunch, and I was sitting alone. She came outside to join me. I saw that she had brought with her a red cardboard box that had once contained my old "Spill and Spell" game.

She held it out to me and said, "You should have this."

Her jewelry, I thought.

Instead, I found within the box a small, worn brown leather portfolio about the size of a paperback book. And within the portfolio, I found dozens of letters and postcards, some written in barely legible, tiny, cramped handwriting, others in beautiful italic script, some dashed off in blunt pencil scrawls on scraps of ragged paper, all neatly tucked away within the various compartments of the portfolio. "These are my letters from camp," she said.

Letters from camp?

She was a Holocaust survivor.

How could she have received mail?

Who wrote to her? What did they say? Where were those people now?

She spread out the papers before me: dozens of stamp-size Hitlers and thick black swastikas now covered the picnic table. "What do you want to know?" my mother said. I heard an edge of defiance, even anger in her voice, as if my curiosity annoyed her. Had I even spoken any of these questions aloud?

Without warning, I was teetering at the edge of the forbidden territory, not wanting to cause her pain, but feeling as if I would burst with questions, some decades old, and some as unexpected as this pile of papers, their edges lifting slightly with each breath of wind, as if inviting me to turn them over.

That was the day that ended nearly fifty years of silence.

I learned that she had been imprisoned in seven different Nazi forced labor camps. And I learned that saving more than three hundred letters, postcards, and photographs and saving her life were inextricably linked. These were not just pieces of paper: they were proxies for the individuals she loved, friends and family who loved her. She hid them during line-ups, handed them to trusted friends, threw them under a building, even buried them under the ground. I began to understand her logic: the risks she undertook to preserve the letters were nothing compared to the danger she would face if she lost them, because they were her motivation to live. Once liberated, she hid them again for decades, but then ensured their preservation once more by revealing their existence and giving them to me.

These letters have been my constant companions since then—not the jewelry I expected, but a far more precious legacy of history.

My mother recovered from the surgery, and allowed me to continue asking my questions, as if the letters themselves formed a bridge over which we could traverse the past and present. I became a student again. As I learned in conversations with historians and librarians around the world, an archive of this quality and size is extraordinary. That "Spill and Spell" box held hundreds of letters, almost all of which were written to Sala. (A few were addressed to other people and she preserved those, too.)

Sala's experience is inextricably linked to the Nazi labor camps, which have not been as well documented as other aspects of the Holocaust. She and her letters survived because she was designated early in the war as a slave, one of about 50,000 people, mostly from western Poland, who were held captive within the Nazi forced labor camp system known as "Organization Schmelt," which is described in detail in the essay by Debórah Dwork and Robert Jan van Pelt.

At killing centers like Auschwitz, Sala would have been unlikely to preserve any personal possessions at all. Schmelt's forced labor camps were different. Sala was a prisoner and slave for nearly five years, she was hungry and worked under terrible conditions, she was threatened by armed guards and vicious dogs—but the Nazis delivered at least some of her mail through the regular Reich postal system. Even so, the survival of a collection of this size, received by one person and covering the entire period of the war, is remarkable. Other labor camp survivors have told me that they also received letters, but theirs were lost or stolen, or left behind after liberation.

On the day that my mother gave me the letters, I knew immediately that my center of gravity had shifted. It was a profound and complex gift, the transmission of a text from a mother to daughter, a story that I had to reconstruct and understand, and then tell again. The box came with no such demands or instructions, of course; I simply followed my instincts as a reader. What began as a desire to understand my mother's past became a quest. What began as her story became mine, and then converged into history.

Od chwili wyjazdu z Sosnowca.

godz. 7 rano wszyscy stawiliśmy się na ulicy Składo...
...erytaniu listy na stacji. Na peronie czekaliśmy do 11½
...ochane dziewczęta! Jak Wam ten postój opisać. Czy ja wted...
...am? Tak. Śniłam od godz. 5 rano do chwili przyjazdu n...
... O 6 Sala pierwsza do mnie przyszła, słodka moja Sala. (...
...i Was wszyst-kich miałam przy sobie, jak b. drogie był...
...i wszystkie, Sala, Gucia, Bala, Chancia i Hela. Kochan...
...ycie mi mogły zajrzeć trochę głębiej do serca jakie
rozpatrzone, a jednak uśmiech na twarzy był na ile tylko
...ogłam pewnie, i mimo że oczy były pełne łez. Trzeba ...
...iało i odważnie choćby serce miało pęknąć. I pożegnałam
...o starego kochanego tatusia. Kochany mój Ojcze. Czy b.
...gnie za swą drogą, za swą wierność dziewczynę. Tak On
...oj Ojciec płakał jak się ze mną żegnał. Naprawdę. Tez eska
...wich wszystkich moich słodkich dziewczyn ...słyszmy. P...
...dzieć Pocoż... Ale ta przyszłość wykaże..... Helę i Chanci
...e pożegnałam pierwsze, potem Balę, biedne zostały tak
...e ale już musiały odejść to do sklep., zostałam z Guci...
...ere już zostały ze mną aż do wyjazdu. Mamcia! o Tobie
...wisu jeszcze nic nie wspomniałam. Ja na ...bie...

Sala's Story

SALA GARNCARZ WAS BORN IN 1924,

the youngest of the eleven children of Chana and Joseph Garncarz. Her father was a rabbi and teacher. They lived in Sosnowiec, Poland, a city of about 130,000. Close to the German border, Sosnowiec (or Sosnowitz, as it was known during the German occupation) was one of the first cities invaded by the Nazis. A poor family to begin with, the Garncarz family had been reduced by the war to new levels of hunger and fear. An elderly bearded Jew was an irresistible Nazi target, and my grandfather refused to shave. He became a prisoner of their one-room apartment, no longer able to walk in the streets, no longer able to go to the synagogue or to give lessons to his students.

In October 1940, an official letter arrived. Sala's sister Raizel was commanded to report to a work camp. The letter came from the *Judenrat,* the puppet government set up by the Nazis. Raizel's name had been put on a list of potential laborers, selected from the 30,000 Jews of Sosnowiec. The letter ordered Raizel, two years older than Sala, to show up at the train station in three days, where she would be taken to a labor camp for six weeks.

Sala volunteered immediately to go in her sister's place. At sixteen, Sala Garncarz was the baby of the family. Beautiful and daring, she was also the family's most effective advocate. Nighttime forays on the roofs of Sosnowiec brought her into target range of German snipers but enabled her to scrounge an extra ration or two. Despite the danger, she relished the excitement and the opportunity to escape from the grinding poverty and claustrophobia of home. She didn't know what a labor camp was—nobody did—but she knew that it was important for everyone to be working. The letter said that she would be paid.

And whatever this camp might be, she knew that it would be easier for her to adapt than it would be for Raizel, who was timid, deeply religious, and resistant to change.

So Sala made her bold proposal and her parents agreed. None of them ever suspected that six weeks of labor would stretch into almost five years of slavery.

On October 28, 1940, Sala Garncarz reported to the train station. Carrying a small bundle of clothes and accompanied by her mother and her closest friends, Sala joined hundreds of Jews, mostly men, who were milling about the train station, anxious, unhappy, and confused. Armed soldiers were yelling in German. The scene was noisy and chaotic, and her mother wept openly, holding on to Sala.

A few yards away, a woman in her early thirties was watching Sala and her mother. She approached, asked if she might be of assistance. My grandmother spoke little Polish, but through tears she tried to explain to the stranger—tall, elegant, well-spoken—that Sala was her youngest child, and that she was so afraid of sending her into the unknown world. "Don't worry, I'll take care of her," volunteered the stranger. She introduced herself as Ala Gertner. Like a fairy godmother, she soothed my grandmother, who reluctantly let go of Sala and allowed Ala to take her away to join the queue for the train, bound for a labor camp in the small town of Geppersdorf.

So would begin the most important friendship of my mother's life. For the next three years, in person or through her letters, Ala kept her promise to my grandmother.

When they arrived at the camp, Ala was assigned to the central administration, where her typing and language skills were useful. She was a natural leader among the women, and she chose Sala as her closest companion. She arranged for them to share a small room, and she taught Sala how to work the system, whether the goal was improving their living conditions, obtaining special work permits, or staying out of the worst dangers in the camps. They shared confidences, Sala about her frustrations at home and dreams for the future, and Ala about her secret romance with a much younger man at the camp, Bernhard Holtz. Ala dubbed her "Sarenka," the deer, for the grace and speed with which Sala delivered love notes between Ala and Bernhard. Ala also protected the more vulnerable girl: when Nazi doctors visited Geppersdorf, it

Sara Garncarz, twelve years old, Sosnowiec, Poland, 1936.

Sala's parents, Chana and Joseph Garncarz, in the 1920s. Sala kept these two photographs with her throughout the war. *(Courtesy of Ann Kirschner and family)*

The first letter Sala received at the Geppersdorf labor camp. Written by her sister Raizel, it was filled with questions about life in the camp.

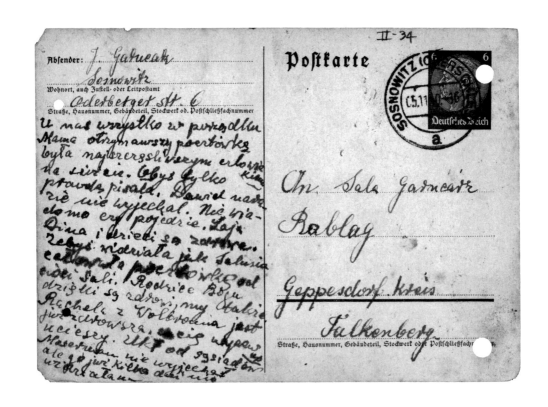

was Ala who hid Sala from the makeshift operating room that sterilized selected prisoners. Not all the women in the camp escaped such treatment.

Sala received her first letter from Raizel within two weeks of her arrival at Geppersdorf.

November 4, 1940

Dear Sister,

We were very happy to get your postcard, as you can well imagine. But Sala, don't think that we stopped worrying just because we received your postcard—nothing of the kind, because you write so little about yourself. Write in more detail. How is the food? What do you eat, when, and do you like the food? Do you cook? Write as often as possible! How are the sleeping arrange-ments? You write that you have separate beds, do you have covers? Do you have heating? We are anxious to know everything. Dear Sala, we certainly want to know everything about you, but one forgets the right thing to ask, so please fill in whatever is missing.

Sala! We did not send a package as yet, because there was no time. We will try to send it, maybe tomorrow, as soon as we find out how....

All is well with us ... when Mother received your postcard, she was the happiest person in the world. May your words only prove to be the truth. As of now, our brother-in-law David remains at home. We don't know if he will leave. [Our sister] Laya Dina and the children are in good health. You should have seen how [our niece] Salusia kissed the postcard from Aunt Sala.

Raizel

Raizel wrote on behalf of the family. In nearly every letter, she included news and greetings from their parents, their sisters Blima and Laya Dina, and Laya Dina's children. She also sent blessings for "dear unknown Miss Ala" for her "thorough care and protection of our sister and daughter." Raizel described the whirl of joy and relief when Sala's letters arrived, but did not hesitate to rebuke Sala frequently: "Our ordeals are beyond words. How can you neglect us by not writing to us for such a long time?"

Frequency of mail was at the discretion of the individual camp director. At Geppersdorf, Sala was allowed to write home every two weeks. Mail and packages were allowed, even encouraged, as if the slave laborers were first-time campers away from home and the Nazis were eager to reassure anxious parents that all was well. No special post was required, although Raizel observed that the mail was processed faster when it was sent through the regular system than when it went through the Jewish post office.

Because mail offered at least some assurance that a loved one was well and working, it was an effective propaganda tool. Most of the envelopes or postcards were reviewed by a censor and then stamped with a "Z" to indicate that they had been cleared. A handful of early letters were written in Polish, but by early 1941 all of Sala's correspondents switched to German, in accordance with Nazi regulations. Later on, they were also required to identify themselves as Jewish by adding "Sara" or "Israel" to their return addresses.

Risking Raizel's wrath, Sala devoted some of her quota of letters to her close group of girlfriends. They too were clamoring for her attention. Their talk of boyfriends and photographs and haircuts helped to connect her to the teenage world that she had so recently shared.

January 20, 1941

Dear Sala,

We read the postcard you sent to your parents.... Why don't you write a special note to us? Didn't you get our letter? What is new with you, what do you do? Write everything.... There is nothing new with us, time goes quickly, as it usually does. Only we miss you, and would very much like to see you and to know what you look like now. We'd be happy to get you the photo you asked [us] for, and told your parents about it. All of us had pictures taken, but when you come home and see us, you will have a lot to laugh about, because one looks worse than the other....

Sala [Rabinowicz], Gucia, Bela, Chana

Geppersdorf belonged to a group of labor camps known informally as RAB or *ReichsAutoBahnLager,* which were extending the German highway to the east, in accordance with construction contracts negotiated by Organization Schmelt with private German businesses. The Geppersdorf Jews had been designated for the firms of Mathies and Moll.

Amid the fears and deprivations of
occupied Poland, on March 27, 1941,
Raizel writes of a moment of celebration,
the engagement of their older sister Blima.

419

Mazel tow   I   Mazel tow

Sosnowitz den 27/III 41r.

Teure Salu!

Halb zehn frie. Ich geh an der straße.
Indem... Es geht der post träger.
Er geht herunter № 9. Ich geh zu
zu ihm, Fileicht hat er für uns
etwas, das herz hat mir gesagt, oder
er will nicht geben, ich soll warten.
Ich habe folkom ferzichtet zu gehn
an der strase, ich muss sich etwas
derwarten. habe sich nicht genart. Wie
nur er ist zugekommen zu unser haus
hat er mich schon arosgehert und was
für ein überraschung 2 post karten mit
einmal. Stell sich for was für uns
das bedeutet. Ich habe sie mitgenommen
mit sich zu lesen. Nu ——— ferstehst
selbst wie auf mir das gewirkt hat wegen
K. B. auf der lekeje bin ich gewesen

Mazel tow

Mazel tow

The women worked mostly in the kitchen and laundry. Sala had been apprenticed as a seamstress at an early age to her sisters and brothers, and volunteered to sew and mend for the officers. She worked on German uniforms but also on personal requests, making a sheepskin motorcycle seat for one officer, sewing doll's clothes for the granddaughter of another. Lacking a machine at Geppersdorf, the Nazis commandeered the sewing machine of local Germans, the Pachta family.

A guard drove Sala every day to the Pachta family's home to use their machine. It did not take long before she was treated like a second daughter to Anna Pachta and her husband, Wilhelm, and a sister to their daughter, Elfriede. The family photographs included another member of the family, a young son, but he was apparently away from home, and was rarely discussed. The family stuffed her with food, gave her clothing, sent money to her parents, even mailed a wooden doll to Sosnowiec as a gift for Sala's niece, Salusia. On May 21, 1941, Raizel wrote to Sala of the gift: "Salusia plays with her baby doll very carefully: she's afraid to disturb it. She asked me to thank you. And please thank the Pachta family for sending it. Even more thanks to them from dear mother for their conscientious supervision, and best regards to them from us all. May God repay them for their care of you."

Elfriede Pachta and her family were local Germans who befriended Sala during her time at the Geppersdorf labor camp.

Elfriede Pachta proved to be as daring as Sala: one fine spring day, she conceived of a grand adventure for the two of them. Removing the blue and white armband that identified Sala as a Jew, Elfriede took her friend on a forbidden visit to the nearby town. The two girls promenaded around the village square, Sala terrified at the potential consequences but exhilarated by the rare and cherished hour of freedom.

Eventually, the camp received its own sewing machine. The Pachtas and Sala cried at being separated, but they continued to visit her at the camp. As the camp grew larger, security increased, and barbed wire encircled the camp.

The Pachta family encountered greater scrutiny from the camp guards. The visits stopped.

After a year at Geppersdorf, rumors began to fly about "vacations" for the forced laborers. Raizel alternated between hope and despair, but when Ala herself showed up, Raizel allowed herself to be optimistic.

September 11, 1941

Dearest Sala,

What is there to write when you are coming home any day now? If only you could stay, then you'd still get something out of life.

We received your card today and I never saw father cry so much. When I started reading it aloud, I couldn't believe what I was reading and I choked on my tears, father started crying terribly, mother and Blima, too, it was a terrible sight.

The holidays will be here soon and I know that you, my sister, wish to spend the time with us and you hope for a better life than you have had until now. How well you expressed that hope, Sala, and we all agree. Understand that we talk day and night of nothing but you and how much, how much we long to enclose you in our arms.

Yesterday I met Ala. We talked for a while and she said that everything will be all right and she consoled me by saying, "you will see, you will soon be together with your daughter and sister."

May you always be with us.

Raizel

Their dream came true. Sala did return home for three days. She balanced her time between friends and family, resigned to the hopeless sense of conflict governing every precious second of her time. She saw Ala only briefly, but they visited a local photography studio, where the camera captured a moment of deep love as the older woman and the young girl gazed into each other's eyes.

Ala secured a job with Moshe Merin, the head of the local Jewish Council, and was allowed to extend her furlough indefinitely. But she could not help her dear "Sarenka," and Sala's family had no money for bribes, no strings to

Ala Gertner and Sala Garncarz in
Sosnowiec, September 1941. This
photograph was taken while Sala
was home from the labor camp on a
three-day "vacation" to visit her family.

pull. Sala believed what she had been told: if she did not return to Geppersdorf, no one else would be allowed to leave the camp.

Joseph Garncarz blessed his youngest child, and said, "I will not see you again." The fiction that she would be away for six weeks was long over. Sala went back to Geppersdorf alone. She never saw her parents or Ala again.

The letters resumed as soon as she returned. She missed Ala terribly, but now she began to receive mail from her as well.

September 24, 1941

Sarenka, you silly girl,

I know, you were disappointed, but I couldn't help myself. I know that I spent little time with you when you were home, but you have to understand why. To begin with, the vacation was short. Then my work, going home, even the bad weather, everything interfered this time.

But don't think badly of me, and don't lose hope. There is no reason why you shouldn't trust me. I felt your reticence quite keenly. There is, Sarenka, no excuse. You are younger and should have a little more understanding of etiquette toward your elders. We can't always say what we want to say, or all we want to say. In the camp, I protected you and surrounded you with warmth. You miss my caring, certainly, my golden precious, but Sosnowitz is different; and besides, I was in an unusual position. I hope that you will get to know me better—those you know and those you don't know yet. Everything in its own time. The next time, Sala.

But now you have to be a good girl. Don't cry and pout. Who can and will understand me, if you act in such a foolish way? You're silent—why? Write what you think, including the most minute details. Don't be afraid, I always think of your release, just be patient.

I have remained the same Ala, even though I have so many possibilities and opportunities to become someone <u>else</u>. I am amazed myself: to be as attached to the camp as I am, is rare. Believe me, Sarenka, I am very sorry that you didn't stay with me. Do you remember the hours on Saturday when you came into my bed early in the morning? We amused and puzzled [everybody].

You wrote very well about how you feel about the camp. Sarenka, are you still in such a pessimistic mood? I consider myself lucky to have so much work. In this way, day after day passes quickly.... I ordered skin cream for you, I'll send it together with the photos the next time.

A postcard to Sala on August 15, 1941, written
by both her sister Raizel and her friend Ala
Gertner while Ala was visiting Sala's family.

A scribbled note from Ala to Sala, December
23, 1940. Older and more experienced, Ala
helped her much younger friend Sala to adjust
to the routine of the labor camp.

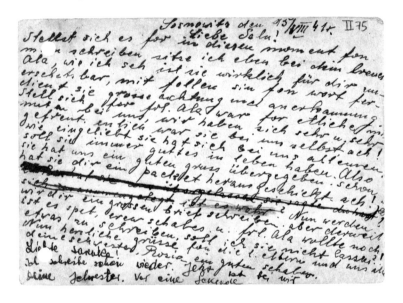

By the fall of 1941, Ala had returned home. In this note she reflects fondly on the time that she and Sala were together at the camp and urges her young friend to have patience while she tries to arrange for Sala's release.

Written on a torn scrap of paper, reflecting the increasing wartime shortages, this note from Ala on December 10, 1941, indicates that she has sent pajamas and a warm nightgown. "Yesterday I ironed my laundry, but you are better at it."

Sarenka, keep trusting me, I kiss you, as always, you beautiful girl.
Give regards to all the women. Write me, clearly and in detail, okay?

Yours, Alinka

One day, Sala received a summons to report to the head of the camp. She had been reckless of late. Just that morning, she had thrown down a swastika armband in front of a guard who had mocked her sewing skills. Ala had warned her against taking such risks. Assuming that she had finally gone too far, she said goodbye to her friends and entered the office believing that she was about to be beaten or killed. As she feared, an unfamiliar SS officer was waiting. Instead of the bullet she expected, he reached down and held out a package to her. Inside the package was food and warm clothing ... a gift from the Pachta family. This was the son they rarely spoke about, an SS officer who had tracked her down at his parents' request!

A group of Jewish men and women from the Laurahutte labor camp, 1942. At the center, in a white coat, is Dr. Wolf Leitner. He is holding a doll that belonged to the granddaughter of one of the Nazi guards, who commissioned Sala to sew doll clothes for Christmas.

As the news from home grew darker, and the silences between the letters even longer, Sala's spirits were renewed by this unexpected evidence that there was a world outside the camps, and that her existence still mattered, even if the messenger was an SS officer.

After almost two years at Geppersdorf, Sala was transferred to six different camps between July and December 1942. The Schmelt labor camps were being consolidated. While she had no control over her movements, she continued to be relatively lucky, always managing to stay one step ahead of the transfer that was most to be feared: Auschwitz. These five months were the time of greatest danger for her and for her letters; searches were more frequent and she needed to find new hiding places in each camp. She lost contact with the Pachta family as her location kept changing, and received fewer letters from home. Through her work at the Jewish government office, Ala managed to keep track of Sala's whereabouts, and in one of her letters, she enclosed the photograph that was taken during their brief vacation.

Sala was already a veteran. Her survival skills were sharpened because she had been imprisoned early in the war, and she was young and strong and intuitive. As she moved around, she encountered guards she had met before, and officers who appreciated her sewing skills and tolerated her defiance and daring, or who were even perhaps amused by her outspokenness. They called her the "one clean Jew," since she was the only one who was trusted to handle their uniforms and personal items.

Soon, Sala had a new source of emotional support. She met Harry Haubenstock in Gross Paniow, another of the Schmelt labor camps. Many prisoners were sick with typhus; work was suspended and the camp was quarantined. Sala and Harry remained healthy, and in this slightly relaxed atmosphere they fell in love. Born in Czechoslovakia, Harry had worked in his family's lumber business before the war. Ardent, protective, and jealous, Harry shared his dreams, his stories of his family, even his baby pictures with his "young bride."

October 1942

My dearest little Sala,

You are an interesting person here in the camp…. Sometimes, I hardly know what to say because everybody seems to have their own ideas about you….

Believe me, most precious little Sala, that I hardly recognize myself any longer. I have changed so much and if someone were to see me now, they would hardly believe that I should be capable of such a deep and sincere love. But I'm glad about this change because this is what my dear parents wished for me. I would be the happiest person on earth, if I had an opportunity to introduce you to my dear parents and to meet yours.

My sweet Salusia, I'm afraid that you will be sad again because I'm writing about our dear parents, but these days I'm thinking of our loved ones every day. Salusia, sweetie, please be so good as to write me today. We will still see each other today at the food distribution.

Sala, I'm closing now and remain, with a thousand kisses

Harry

Sala and Harry Haubenstock in the
Gross Paniow labor camp. Harry wears
the Star of David on his jacket.

Letter from Harry Haubenstock to Sala,
July 1942, in Gross Paniow.

I. VI 28l

Ich hoffe liebste Salusia,
dass noch alles gut wird u.
wir zusammenbleiben wer-
den. Am besten wäre trotz-
dem für uns mit einem
Transport entweder nach
Zinglau od. nach ...
zu fahren, wenn dort diesen
Mädchen kommen möchten.
Salusia, süsse teure, ich
werde nicht aufhören zu
kämpfen, aber man arbei-
tet sehr stark gegen mich.
Du ... Dir schon denken
können wer. Aber ich hoffe
dass wir doch lieber bleiben
werden.
Ich möchte ja gerne

But when the quarantine ended, so did their relative freedom, and letters and meetings became more dangerous. They both knew that transports were being arranged. Harry managed to get them transferred together from Gross Paniow to Blechhammer, another Schmelt camp, but they were then separated after a few weeks. They would meet in Prague after the war, Harry promised, and they would marry.

In late 1942, Harry was sent to Dyhernfurth, a factory that produced poison gas. Sala's next, and last, camp was in Schatzlar, a remote ski village in the mountains on the border of Poland and Czechoslovakia. A few hundred Jewish women worked there in a cotton-processing factory, a *spinnerei*. The factory continued to operate on the business principles of the Schmelt camps, even though the camp was now administratively part of the Gross Rosen concentration camp. All pretense of payment to the workers had long since been abandoned. The Schatzlar factory was owned by the Buhl Sohne textile company, and the German manager lived across the street from the factory with his wife and children.

Sala brought her stack of papers with her, including the thirty love letters she had received from Harry. For her birthday in 1943, she received one last letter from him, in which he enclosed his most valuable possession: a photograph of the two of them that had been taken in the Gross Paniow labor camp, Harry's yellow star clearly visible on his suit, Sala smiling shyly next to him.

Raizel and the rest of the Garncarz family remained in Sosnowiec until the spring of 1942. Even for the prolific Raizel, letters were becoming harder to compose without frightening Sala or risking censorship. Writing more in code, Raizel hinted at the true state of the family's situation. Work and food were impossible to find. Deportations had become an everyday nightmare; Raizel alludes to these often violent confrontations as "weddings" to which she had not been invited. "You're so right, Sala, to thank God that our address is still the same," she said. Their mother had been seriously ill, and one of Laya Dina's children developed pneumonia.

Raizel's handwriting betrayed her rising anxiety. Instead of carefully composed, neatly written letters and postcards, some in beautiful calligraphy, she wrote in haste, and no longer filled the pages with her elegant, almost leisurely prose.

Despite the worsening situation, Raizel's faith remained strong. She wrote more than one hundred letters to her sister, and almost every one was infused with religious belief. Her demands that Sala should be equally steadfast, regardless of the alien circumstances of the labor camp, were far more than sisterly reminders: Raizel held herself accountable to the highest standard of religious observance, and she could demand no less of her sister: "Remember that there is one God." She marked the passage of time by the Jewish calendar, although each Sabbath, each holiday, brought a fresh and mournful reminder of their sad circumstances. She assured Sala that even during the Passover of 1942 she ate no bread and lamented the perversion of a family gathering where the chairs were empty, and the plates were bare.

Sosnowitz, April 1, 1942

Dear Sala,

Just now, I'm in the post office writing. My heart is bleeding, because we didn't send you matzo. Oh God! Can you believe this? It's the night before the [Passover] holiday, and there are no matzos, no ... nothing. I can tell you, we're more than happy because you don't have to be with us today. You wouldn't be as bothered anyway: nothing pulls you down as easily as it does us.

It looks like [the fast of] Yom Kippur, the candles are lit, the table cloth is on the table. I'd much rather not write you all that much, just let me say, be happy, happy, merry and gay. Laugh as much as you can. For we do the same here at home. I even wrote you a letter, but Father, may he live long, didn't allow me to send it. I'm sure all of you there are laughing not knowing what to do and, I'm sure, you're crying too. May it be for the best, keep on laughing. Sala, remember, don't worry about us. Have a good time ... Sala, have a good time....

Raizel

In May, the entire family was caught in a round-up, but then allowed to return home—all except Sala's brother, who was deported to a labor camp.

Dear Sala,

    I guess, you'll be impatient by now, but what can I do? My head keeps spinning, my head, it's just awful, but Sala, don't worry about us, we're home. How lucky you are! Be happy, be glad and thank God a thousand times every day that you still have somebody to whom you can write, with the way things are going here.... But don't worry about that.

    [Our brother] Moshe David was sent off to work today. He should have come to your place but he'll be sent somewhere else. Don't worry about his wife and children, they are fine. Not to worry, everything is fine here. What's new with you? Sala, remember how lucky you are, you have no idea. Enough now, it's already late, time to sleep, one is tired after a long day.

    Good night. Write more about yourself, not about us.

        Raizel

Around August 12, 1942, the whole family was again taken from home, but this time the catastrophe was complete. According to eyewitness accounts and historical documents, an estimated 50,000 Jews from Sosnowiec and the neighboring region were herded to an open sports field, where they stood for days without food or facilities, in the heat of summer and through a torrential rainstorm, while Nazis proceeded with the gigantic selection. On August 19, 1942, the two sisters, Raizel and Blima, were sent to the line for forced laborers; a third sister, Laya Dina, was able to show working papers for herself and her husband, and was allowed to return home.

In a letter that I can never read without weeping, my aunt Raizel describes her separation from my grandparents.

        August 25, 1942

Dear Sala,

    I am sure you are wondering where we got this address in Neusalz from, but it's for real. That's what happened. Blima [and I and some of your friends from home] are together. Fate has brought us here. Thank God, we're not doing badly. Don't worry about us. But we're worried about our dear, precious, precious parents. We don't know what happened to them. May God give us some good news.

Letter from Raizel from the Neusalz labor
camp, to which she and Blima were sent
in August 1942. Their parents later went
to their deaths at Auschwitz.

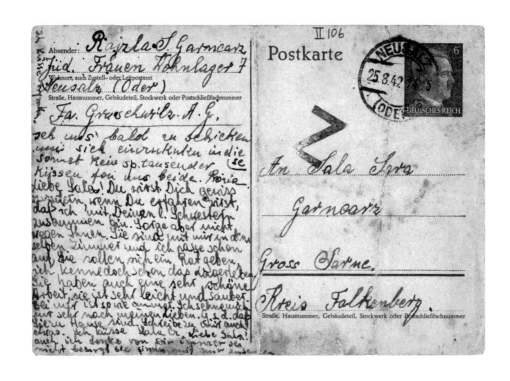

Laya Dina and David apparently returned home. On the last day, on August 19, we saw Laya Dina on the way to the station, which reassured us somewhat. But we didn't see our parents. May they be well.

Sala, Sala you are the best. We're always holding your picture in our hands and keep talking about you. If you have more than one photo of our parents, please send it to us. Otherwise, there's nothing else to say. A thousand kisses from both of us.

Raizel

About 10,000 Jews who could not work because they were too old, too young, or too weak were sent by train to Auschwitz. Among them were my grandparents.

Laya Dina and her family were evicted again from their apartment and crowded into the ghetto. "I haven't had an apartment for four weeks," she wrote to Sala. "Throughout these four weeks I was crazy, really crazy. Wherever you spend the night, you don't spend the day."

"May God grant that I don't have to write Him a postcard for all of us, sisters and parents, to be able to sit together at a table and rejoice," Laya Dina wrote, before she too fell silent.

A few more letters from Ala trickled through. She was still working in the office of Moshe Merin, the Jewish governor, and the official stamps on her letters may have helped her chances of getting through to Sala. She married Bernhard Holtz, her boyfriend from Geppersdorf. But Ala's luck ran out in July 1943. The liquidation of Sosnowiec and its neighboring cities was in its final stage. Merin himself and his closest associates were summoned to the offices of the Gestapo and never returned. In this last letter, mailed from the ghetto at Bedzin, Ala's optimism is undiminished, although it is hard to imagine that she did not know that her next destination was Auschwitz.

July 16, 1943

Dearest Sarenka,

Suddenly, I'm here at the post office. The mail is going out today and how could I not write to my Sarenka? Just now, my husband, Bernie was here. He looks good and feels well. I'm curious about how you are, how your health is. We are well and plan to go to the camp. Today is a gorgeous day, we are in the best of spirits and have great hopes for the future.

What's doing with Harry? Where is he? Why is he silent? Don't worry, girl, it'll be fine. Be brave, stay well. Kisses,

your little Ala

Ala was assigned to the Union munitions factory, one of the most coveted work details at Auschwitz-Birkenau because its members received more rations and better treatment. News from the outside world filtered in even here, overheard from the guards, who were increasingly nervous about the progress of the war, or from inmates transferred from other camps. By the end of 1944, they could see Allied war planes overhead.

In the belief that the Germans would kill them soon, the men of the *Sonderkommando*, the Jewish prisoners who worked at the crematoria, planned an armed rebellion. They had a few guns, and hoped that they could obtain explosives in order to build homemade bombs. The only possible source was the inner sanctum of the munitions factory, the closely guarded *Pulverraum,* the Gunpowder Room, where a small group of women worked to fill shell casings with gunpowder.

Ala became one of the key links between the women and the Sonderkommando. She recruited some of the women from the Gunpowder Room, and she passed the smuggled grains of gunpowder to her friend Roza Robota, who was one of the few women who had access to the men's camp. From Roza, the gunpowder was sent along to the Sonderkommando.

On October 7, 1944, the Sonderkommando used the hidden gunpowder supplied by the women to blow up Crematorium IV. For a precious hour or two, chaos reigned throughout the camp, in what appears to have been the only armed rebellion in Auschwitz. The uprising was rapidly put down by the SS. Hundreds of Sonderkommando were killed in the explosion or shot afterwards.

Furious at the audacity of the uprising, high-ranking Nazi officials in Berlin personally handled the investigation. Although the women at the munitions factory were immediately suspected as the source of the explosives, the suspense dragged on for months, until finally the Nazis identified a few of the possible conspirators. The women knew that they were being closely watched, but there was no escape. Ala was the first to be arrested, and may have been betrayed by a Nazi spy who had infiltrated the factory. She was brutally tortured and, according to some reports, confessed and implicated two other women. The Berlin High Court ordered their execution.

Although the eyewitness accounts and later reconstructions of the uprising are rife with contradictions and unresolved mysteries, the women's heroism is often cited as one of the greatest chapters in Holocaust resistance.

On January 5, 1945, Ala Gertner and Regina Sapirstein were hanged publicly. The gallows had been constructed for maximum visibility in an open area near the factory. The women who worked the day shift were summoned to view the execution, their faces slapped if they tried to close their eyes. Roza Robota and Estucia Wajblum were hanged that evening in front of the night shift.

Auschwitz was evacuated twelve days later.

~~~~~~

One by one, Sala's letterwriters had fallen silent. All correspondence from the outside world had ceased. Sala's only letters in 1944 and 1945 were birthday greetings, passed from one room of the camp to another. Her well-wishers were women she had known now for years. They lived like sisters; they divided rations, kept each other clean from lice, and—most importantly—they renewed each other's spirits and rehearsed the lives they hoped to lead in the future.

These handmade birthday cards and poems looked mostly to the future. Calling Sala "Mrs. Haubenstock," and wishing her the traditional 120 years of health and happiness, Sala's friends helped keep her dreams alive. They crystallized the joy of friendship and sisterhood that she found even in a forced labor camp, visions of freedom and marriage, reunion with beloved parents, and an end to the long season of dread.

March 5, 1945

Dear Sala,

March 5 is a happy and a lucky day for us…. Today we are celebrating our dear Sala's birthday, alas, still behind barbed wire. Oh, what a great holiday this would be if we celebrated your birthday in freedom, together with your loved

die herzlichsten Wünsche zum Geburtstage

1944

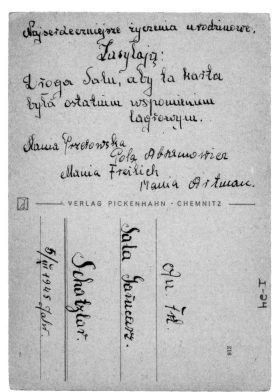

Najserdeczniejsze życzenia urodzinowe.

Zasyłają:

Droga Salu, aby ta karta była ostatnim wspomnieniem lagrowym.

Mania Pretowska

Pola Abramowicz

Mania Freilich

Mania Artman.

VERLAG PICKENHAHN · CHEMNITZ

5/II 1945 Jahr.

Schatzlar.

Sala Garncarz.

An. Frl.

So viel Glück für Dich,
Wieviel Tropfen im See.
Ein Leben im Licht.
Ohne Kampf, ohne Weh.
Ein Leben voll Sonne,
So strahlend wie Edelstein.
Ein Leben voll Wonne
Soll Dir immer beschieden sein.

Das wünschen Dir von ganzem Herzen
Deine Freundinnen Ewa, Sala u. Frieda
den 5. II 1944

An. Frl.

Sala Garncarz

Schatzlar

Sala was in the Schatzlar labor camp for three birthdays: 1943, 1944, and 1945. Each year she received handmade cards and postcards from friends in the camp. The women may have bartered with the local Czech drivers who delivered raw materials to the Schatzlar factory to obtain the cards and pens with which to create original cards.

ones.... Let good luck shine on you just like the bright sunshine that steals secretly through our camp windows....

Sala, sometimes, when the three of us are in the bunk, and you are asleep, we hear you call in your sleep: "Mommy, Daddy ..." We do not want to wake you, for we know that, at that moment, you are happily with them. [We] talk it over: "Should we wake her or not?" ...

Forgive us, Sala dearest, that we sometimes disturb your sweet dreams. Someday, we shall let you drink deeply from the cup of happiness, ... with your parents and with your Harry, when we are free.

Your loving friends

The German Director of the Schatzlar camp knew that time was running out for him too. The pretense that this camp was contributing to the war effort was wearing thin. No trucks or trains were delivering raw materials to the factory. The Director had to find ways to keep the Jews busy, or he too might be sent to the front. In the winter of 1945, he put the women to work digging trenches, under the watchful eyes and guns of SS guards and dogs. Marching out to work each day in the snow without shoes or warm clothes, the women passed by a French prisoner-of-war camp, where the men shouted words of encouragement that the war would soon be over. Allied leaflets began to fall from the sky, exhorting them to courage and patience. Liberation was near.

But the French prisoners of war also warned the women that they might be killed at the last minute to eliminate all traces of the camps. Sala and her friends took turns keeping watch all night, fearful that the guards would throw a hand grenade into the barracks. The women secretly sewed flags of different colors, not knowing which army might arrive first at the camp.

On the night of May 7, the women discovered that they were alone. The guards had disappeared, fleeing into the forest. From their window, the women watched as the Director walked by, carrying heavy cans of gasoline into the house that he shared with his wife and children. He entered and shut the front door. Within minutes, the entire house exploded.

The women selected a handmade red flag to welcome the Russians when they liberated the camp on May 8, 1945.

The circles of Sala's life narrowed continually from 1940 to 1945. But now, they began to widen again.

Although the Russian liberators urged the Jews to take revenge, Sala and her friends wanted only to go home. Without money or identification, unsure as to how this new world worked, the women began to leave the camp immediately. Most of them left all reminders of the camps behind. Only Sala paused to put together her letters. She traveled to Poland with a friend, hitchhiking rides with soldiers on trucks and trains. When she finally reached home, she found no sign of her family. Polish families occupied her apartment, professing total ignorance as to the previous tenants. Trying to hitch a free ride on a local trolley, Sala was thrown off by a conductor who told her that no Jews were welcome.

Sala vowed to leave Poland forever. But where to go? She and Harry had agreed to meet in Prague if they survived, so that would be her next destination. A Russian officer, himself Jewish, befriended Sala and secured her travel to Prague with an escort of Russian soldiers. The Czech people

Telegram from Harry Haubenstock to Sala, July 26, 1945, from Prague.

welcomed the Jewish refugees with free soup and housing, a profound contrast to what they had found in Poland.

She found news of Harry through the informal network of refugees. He had survived! But he sent her a telegram telling her to wait, and then sent someone else in his place to say that he would not marry her. Sala cried, but heeded the advice of her friends to move on. She added Harry's telegram to his love letters and his baby pictures. Her new plan was to immigrate to Israel. But first, she had to be sure that no other survivors remained from her family. She heard that the largest gathering of refugees was at Bergen-Belsen, and she headed there next, traveling in the company of a few friends, riding on top of coal cars on freight trains, hitchhiking, and walking.

Still a few days from Bergen-Belsen, the group came through the pretty Bavarian village of Ansbach. They met some old friends who urged them to stay and celebrate in Ansbach's beautiful synagogue for their first Jewish New Year in freedom since 1940. Ansbach was in the American zone, and the streets were filled with refugees as well as soldiers from the nearby U.S. Army base in Nuremberg.

September 1945: the first Rosh Hashanah after liberation. Every seat in the Ansbach synagogue was filled. A young New Yorker named Sidney Kirschner noticed Sala, and introduced himself after the service. They walked together, conversing in Yiddish, the only language they shared. Despite the mistrust of her friends from camp—none of whom had ever met an American— Sala and Sidney became engaged a few months later. But Sidney's mother, herself an emigrant from Poland, objected to the match.

Sala wrote directly to her prospective mother-in-law, asking for her blessing:

To the mother of Sidney,

Before I took the pen in my hand, I turned it over a few times and I came to the conclusion that I have to do it, it's my obligation. I'm hoping that I'll be properly understood. Ah! If I could only find the proper words ... it's very difficult for me. But I have to do it so that my conscience will be clean and I will never feel guilty. The time is short.

Sidney will return home soon where he's been impatiently awaited. He longs to be home. He and I want the same thing, but it is something I won't and can't accept, something I will not make a decision about, before we get the blessing and acceptance of the mother of Sidney. This is not a child's game, not something you can buy, or something that you can change with time. No! It is a life's problem, a life's question.

Unfortunately, I was not given the happiness of being able to ask my dearest mother for her blessing. The future dealt me heavy blows when it took the holiest and the best from me, to be able to say the word "mother" or to write and ask whether it is right for me to be married.

Sala in front of the Ansbach
synagogue in the fall of 1945.

Sala and Sidney Kirschner in
Ansbach, February 1946.

Telegram from Sidney to his mother in New York discussing plans for a civil wedding ceremony in Europe, to be followed by a religious ceremony in America.

WESTERN UNION
CABLEGRAM

A. N. WILLIAMS
PRESIDENT

CLASS OF SERVICE

This is a full-rate Cablegram unless its deferred character is indicated by a suitable symbol preceding the address.

SYMBOLS

LC	Deferred Cablegram
NLT	Cable Night Letter
	Ship Radiogram

Received at

N2 INTL=CD NURNBERG VIA WU CABLES 67 1

VLT MRS J KIRSCHNER=

2004 THIRDAVENUE NEWYORKVITYNY=

EVERYTHING WORKING OUT FINE GETTING MARRIED EARLY NEXT WEEK
AND LEAVING FOR HOME THE EIGHT THE MARRIAGE WILL BE A CIVIL
AFFAIR I WANT TO LEAVE THE RELIGIOUS CEREMONY FOR HOME
WHEN YOU CAN BE PRESENT ALL IS BEING DONE ACCORDING TO
HOYLE BEST REGARDS TO ALL GIVE MY LOVE TO RAE HOPE TO SEE
YOU REAL SOON LOVE=

=SID=

=2004 HOYLE RAE=

So we acknowledge that this is our obligation, to be waiting and waiting. For what? For your permission. We have not received an answer: why? I can answer this question myself. It is possible that my parents would handle this the same way: we don't really know each other. A child is everything to a mother, especially the youngest child. Like Sidney, I am also the youngest child. We want the best for them, to see everything nicer, bigger, better. And if we don't know where they are going, or with whom they go, so far away, we don't have faith. We are not sure. I can understand and tolerate this, but we have now reached the last minute.

About me, there's nothing much to write—a plain Jewish girl from a kosher home and that's all. I think it's enough. I'm putting my future in this letter. If a positive answer comes, as we hope, then we remain happy. If not, then it's difficult but I'll have to say like a Jew always says, everything is for the best. Whichever way the answer should be, please write and don't pay attention to my words, only answer what your heart and feelings are.

Please forgive that I'm writing in Yiddish and not perfect Yiddish— but one does forget how to write and I don't know English at all.

Sala

Sidney's mother acquiesced, and he returned to the United States to arrange for Sala's passage.

Her joy during this period was further intensified by the knowledge that Raizel and Blima had survived and were convalescing in Sweden.

October 10, 1945

My Beloved Sisters Blima and Rozia,

Unfortunately, fate did not decree that we should finally meet after five years. However, this does not scare me so much any more because I have finally located you, and I hope that we will meet soon. I had already lost all hope that I would find anyone from our family.

I went back home right after the war ended. Alas, our home is no more! I found nobody there, and you can imagine how I felt in my heart when

I entered the main gate. It's best not to write about it ... I left Sosnowiec on the same day, since I could not stay there even a minute longer. We have nobody left, nobody! ...

I was living in Waldenburg, some 800 kilometers from Sosnowiec. An acquaintance came by to tell me about a list from Bergen in Sosnowiec, and that your names are on it. The following day I had a chance to drive to Czechoslovakia but, unfortunately, I had to stop in Prague for three weeks.

Now I reproach myself that maybe I was too late because of that. As I entered the American sector, I found out that you had already left for Sweden. It hit me like a bolt of lightning but, at the same time, I was glad to have the assurance that you are alive....

I have the pictures of our dear father and dear mother, together with all the mail I received from home, starting from the first minute that I left for camp. All along, I watched it and guarded it like the eyes in my head, since it was my greatest treasure.

... Do remember that I am waiting impatiently, for any news from you. Personally, I don't know what to write anymore as it is so hard to remember everything. Please write to me and let me know who is still with you.... Meanwhile, I will bid you farewell.

I kiss you both warmly.

Your sister Sala

Raizel's letters began again.

December 6, 1945

Dearest newly found little sister,

My hands are trembling. I am jumping around, going crazy: I am delirious. I don't know where to begin. So my intuition concerning you was correct, after all, and you are alive for us! My mind is frantic, confused. December 6, 1945 will be a memorable, festive one for us, for today I received a letter from you, my dearest one. I can't believe my eyes; it happened just as I was feeling abandoned and resigned. I did not doubt that you were alive, but I could not figure out how you—the one of us who knew best how to survive—remained silent. Why doesn't she let us hear from her, I thought to myself. Forgive me, Sala, for writing so inco-

herently. Oh God, what goes on in my mind now! My love, I read your letter ten times. My tears covered up your words, so [others] had to help me read them, while I tried to calm myself.

... Dearest one. Now that I know you are alive, I must work twice as hard to get well quickly, so that when I am healthy and strong, I will be ready to see you, looking well too. Finally, after all our sufferings, after six years of horror and separation, we will be able to hug you tight, close to our heart.

Sala, I do not wish to, and will not write to you about our experiences, because no matter how much I write, it could not, would not measure up to the reality of it all. I want to talk to you, face to face, about everything. When will that be, Sala?

... Once more, we live for your letters. Even when we had no news about you, I kept staring at the door—as if I knew for certain that you were about to arrive. And now you have appeared again on earth's surface! Hold to it fast, fast, so you can recapture at least a bit of your lost young life.

December 20, 1945

... It is 12 o'clock now on Friday. I see our dear mother fussing in the kitchen to prepare for Shabbat, our father also getting ready to welcome a guest.... Ah, that's all my imagination. I wish I had at least a picture, so that I could at least be able to kiss his high forehead and his long gray beard. When you came home the first and only time from camp to see us, it was also on a Friday. How happy we all were and how quickly it passed by. How hopeful our dear father was to see you still alive. I had to read your letters ten times for him. He was so sorry to put them away.... Sala, I cannot see his figure, but his voice comes to me again.

... May God grant our wish that someone else from our family will be found....

Your sister Raizel

There were no other survivors.

Raizel and Blima came to the United States and settled in Brooklyn, New York. Both married, but neither had children. Blima died in 1953, her heart weakened by her ordeal in the camps. Raizel became a beloved teacher in Borough Park, Brooklyn. She died in 2002.

I find the timetable of Sala's new life breathtaking. She was liberated in May. By July, she had traveled to Sosnowiec, and to Prague, where her hope of finding family and reunion with Harry was smashed. She met Sidney in September, was engaged by January, and in March she was married in a civil ceremony in Germany. By May, just a little over a year after liberation, she and hundreds of other war brides were headed for New York aboard the USS *George Goethals*. She was married again, this time by a rabbi, on June 8, 1946. She was wearing a wedding gown that was borrowed from a recent bride by Sidney's ever practical mother. Sala had no family, no friends, at her wedding.

Sala in Central Park, New York City, reading the Yiddish-language *Jewish Daily Forward*, 1946.

She settled in New York. Somewhere in the three-room East Harlem apartment that she and Sidney shared with his mother, Sala hid the box of letters. And said nothing about them, not about the letters, not about her life during the war, for nearly fifty years.

Sala was carried away on a tidal wave of history in which she could have been simply one more victim. But she made three choices that shaped her life: She volunteered to go to the camp in her sister's place. She embraced as her mentor the incomparable Ala Gertner. And she nurtured a collection of letters, believing that only they could sustain her individuality and humanity amidst the degradation and death of the camp.

A few months ago, I asked my mother what she expected when she gave me the letters. "Nothing in particular," she said. "I just didn't want you to find them when I wasn't alive, when you wouldn't know what they had meant to me." Had she kept her secret, I would never have known the young girl she had been, would never have heard the voices of the writers who kept her alive, would have lost forever the opportunity to engage the precious memories of the survivors as my guide to this complex jigsaw puzzle.

I have often wished that someone had saved Sala's side of the correspondence. Imagine then how unexpected and wonderful it was that ten years after the first letters were revealed, we found additional documents hidden in yet another box in Sala's closet, including fragments of a diary written by the sixteen-year-old Sala during the first few weeks in the camps.

Until then, I knew the young Sala only through her portrayal in the letters of her friends and family, and by her recollections. But now, as if she had been waiting in the wings, she stepped to center stage, recording the first few weeks of her five-year journey, which began at the train station. I see her at sixteen, staring at the strange scene through her luminous gray eyes, assessing her future with a sharp awareness of her need for something else that she could hardly define.

October 28, 1940

From the time of departure from Sosnowiec

At 7:00 o'clock AM, we all arrived at Skladowa Street. After our names were checked, we went to the railroad station where we waited until 11:00 AM. How can I describe this waiting period? Was I dreaming? Yes, I had been dreaming, from 5:00 o'clock in the morning until we arrived at the designated location. By 7:00 o'clock, I had you all with me, all my dear, beloved [friends].

My dearests! If you could have looked deep into my heart, you would have seen how desperate I was; still I tried to keep a smile on my face as best I could, though my eyes were filled with tears. One must go on bravely and courageously, even if the heart is breaking.

I said goodbye to my beloved old father. Dear father, will you miss your Sala a lot? Me, the intolerable girl? My father cried ... yes, he did cry when we were saying goodbye. Onward. Accompanied by all my sweet girlfriends, we started out. Where to? Why? Only the future will tell.

Mother dearest, I have not mentioned you until now. I was not looking at you, though I was consumed by you. You were pleading with me, you were begging me, almost yelling at me—yet, mother, I want to do what I want to do. Now it's so hard to say goodbye; what can I say to you, what to wish you?

The first page of a diary that Sala began on October 28, 1940, covering her departure from Sosnowiec and the first few weeks in the Geppersdorf labor camp.

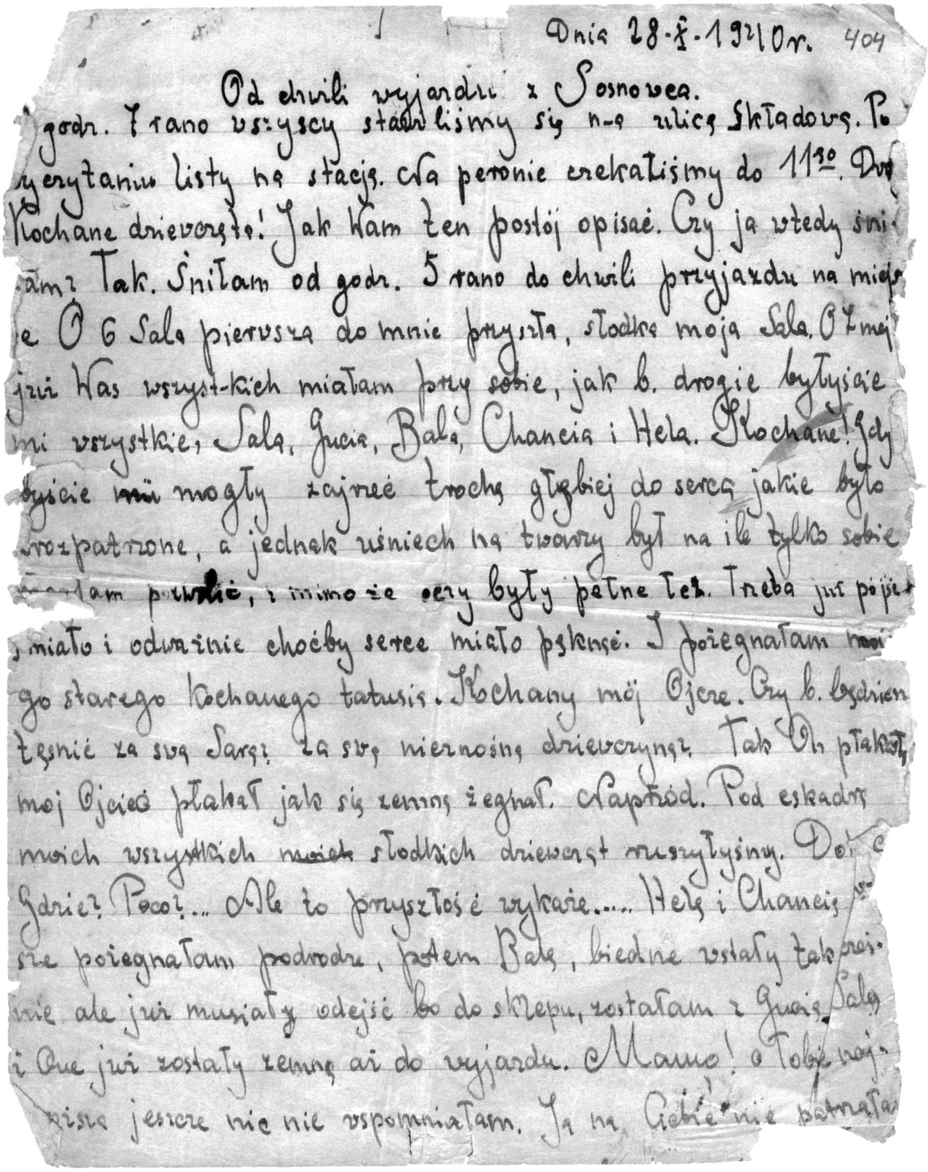

Dnia 28-X-1940 r. 404

Od chwili wyjazdu z Sosnowca.

godz. 7 rano wszyscy staliśmy się na ulicę Składową. Po
czytaniu listy na stację. Na peronie czekaliśmy do 11^30. Dro
Kochane dziewczęta! Jak Wam ten postój opisać. Czy ja wtedy śni
am? Tak. Śniłam od godz. 5 rano do chwili przyjazdu na miejs
e. O 6 Sala pierwsza do mnie przyszła, słodka moja Sala. O 7 mej
już Was wszystkich miałam przy sobie, jak b. drogie byłyście
mi wszystkie, Sala, Gucia, Bala, Chancia i Hela. Kochane! Gdy
byście mogły zajrzeć trochę głębiej do serca jakie było
rozpatrzone, a jednak uśmiech na twarzy był na ile tylko sobie
ałam pozwolić, i mimo że oczy były pełne łez. Trzeba już pójść
miało i odważnie choćby serce miało pęknąć. I pożegnałam mo
go starego kochanego tatusia. Kochany mój Ojcze. Czy b. często
tęsknić za swą Sarą? Za swą niezmożną dziewczyną. Tak Oh płakał
mój Ojciec płakał jak się ze mną żegnał. Naprzód. Pod eskadrą
moich wszystkich słodkich dziewcząt musztyłyśmy. Do
Gdzie? Poco?... Ale to przyszłość wykaże..... Helę i Chancię
sze pożegnałam podrodze, potem Balę, biedne wstały tak wcze
nie ale już musiały odejść bo do sklepu, zostałam z Gucią, Salą
i One już zostały ze mną aż do wyjazdu. Mamo! o Tobie naj
pisze jeszcze nic nie wspominałam. Ja na Ciebie nie patrzała

I said nothing. I did not wish you anything, did not ask you for anything. Still, I could not stop looking at you, mother, because I felt something inside of me tearing, hurting. One more kiss, one more hug. My mother does not want to let go of me. Let it end already, it is torture. I say goodbye to my sisters.

I step into the line-up, and looking around me, I see my faithful friends standing at a distance since they are not allowed to stay too close. Except for my mother and sisters, here everybody and everything are strangers to me.

With whom are you leaving me, and to whom are you sending me off?

Dear girls!!! I am closer to you than even to my sisters, and now I must leave you and go into the unknown world. Will I ever see all of you again? Does it seem possible that I will not be in your house tomorrow? ... I wonder if you will remember me, or talk about me. But what right do I have to demand it?

We are starting to move. Goodbye everybody; remember me, only please do not pity me, because nobody forced me to do this. I got what I wanted. God help me!!

Sala's Europe
1939–1945

N

Rattvik

SWEDEN

LITHUANIA

Bergen-Belsen

Berlin

German
Invasion
(Sept. 1–5, 1939)

Warsaw

GERMANY

Neusalz

POLAND

Lublin

GENERAL
GOUVERNEMENT

Schatzlar

UPPER
SILESIA

Bedzin

Geppersdorf

Prague

Sosnowiec

Krakow

Nuremberg

Auschwitz

Ansbach

FRANCE

CZECHOSLOVAKIA

ZAGLEMBIE

Vienna

AUSTRIA

HUNGARY

Sala's World, 1939–1945:
Sosnowiec, Schmelt's Camps, and the Holocaust

by Debórah Dwork and Robert Jan van Pelt

SALA GARNCARZ, AGED SIXTEEN,
VOLUNTEERED TO TAKE HER SISTER RAIZEL'S PLACE WHEN THE
OLDER GIRL WAS SUMMONED BY THE GERMANS TO WORK IN A
FORCED LABOR CAMP.

We know about Sala's experiences because she survived to relate them. We
know about them, too, because some three hundred letters written to her, as
well as fragments of a diary she kept, survived as well.

This unique cache of documents challenges the common perception of the Holocaust, when Jews disappeared into "the night and fog" without
trace. Millions did indeed disappear into camps where they were murdered
upon arrival. And of the hundreds of thousands whom the Germans permitted
to live, vanishingly few ever received mail. Sala's letters shine a bright light
on the existence of camps where, for a time, Jewish inmates were permitted
to receive letters and from which some inmates were even allowed to return
to the ghettos from which they had come. These so-called Schmelt camps,
named for SS-Oberführer Albrecht Schmelt, Special Representative of the
Reichsführer-SS (Heinrich Himmler) for the Deployment of Foreign Labor in
East Upper Silesia, arose from a particular set of circumstances.[1]

When the Nazis came to power in Germany in 1933, they pursued
their antisemitic agenda relentlessly. Relying, at first, on individual emigration,
they threw Jews out of their jobs, seized Jewish-owned businesses, and made it
impossible for Jewish families to earn a living. Facing poverty and no prospects
for a better future, many German Jews left. The Anschluss of Austria in 1938
gained the Nazis territory they wanted and Jews they didn't. Berlin took matters

more firmly into its own hands, and sent Adolf Eichmann to Vienna to organize the mass emigration and depredation of Austrian Jews. Again the Nazi
strategy was successful. In total, of the 800,000 Jews who in 1933 lived within
the area that in September 1939 was to comprise the Greater German Reich
(Germany, Austria, Sudetenland, and Bohemia and Moravia), more than 450,000
emigrated. The German invasion of Poland from the west and, in accordance
with a secret agreement with the USSR, the Soviet invasion from the east
changed the situation, however. For while the Nazis once more got land they
wanted, there now was nowhere to send the more than two million Jews under
German control, 550,000 of whom lived in areas annexed by Germany and
1.5 million in rump Poland, the so-called General Gouvernement, an area that
included Warsaw, Krakow, Kielce, and Lublin. The war had effectively closed
all national borders. How, the Nazis wondered, were they going to "solve" the
"Jewish problem"? Emigration had become nearly impossible; a new solution
was wanted.[2]

  In a conversation with party ideologue Albert Rosenberg, Hitler
unfolded his vision for Poland and the Jews. He intended to divide the German
share of Poland in three, he explained. The eastern area between the Vistula and
Bug rivers would be reserved "for the whole of Jewry (from the Reich as well) as
well as all other unreliable elements." Hitler's plan, Rosenberg wrote in his diary,
was to Germanize and colonize the western part. In the middle, the Poles were
to be allowed some kind of homeland, at least for the time being.[3]

  Implementation of this "territorial solution" fell to Reinhard
Heydrich, chief of the secret police, who considered the details. To facilitate
deportation of Jews to that eastern area, they needed to be concentrated in
cities "which are either railway junctions or at least lie on a railway line." The
Germans wasted no time: Jews in the General Gouvernement were swept into
such cities from the countryside. Adolf Eichmann, mastermind of the forced
mass emigration process in Vienna, took it from there. He identified an area
around the town of Nisko in Lublin district that he thought would serve nicely
as a reservation, and he planned for the relocation of some two million Jews.
But the sheer mechanics of moving so many people, as well as objections by
the Wehrmacht (German army) command (which had begun to use the area
as a staging ground for mobilization against the Soviet Union) stymied the
project. In the end, some 95,000 Jews were moved to Nisko. Many died. None

of the surviving deportees was allowed to return. The "territorial solution" to the "Jewish problem" had failed.[4]

What to do? The Germans wished to be rid of Jews in the German East, but where to send them? After the Nisko fiasco, ghettoization, which had been instituted in annexed Poland, seemed the least problematical course. Thus, Jews in the General Gouvernement and Jews in those regions that had been annexed to the Reich lived in a limbo situation of enclosed ghettos while the Germans decided what to do with them. The Jews had no way of knowing they were in limbo; they thought that the harsh conditions of the ghetto constituted the Nazis' "solution" to their "Jewish problem."[5]

Local variations and exceptions obtained, however, even in areas annexed to the Reich. Sala Garncarz and her family lived in such a region. Their city, Sosnowiec, was located in Zaglembie, which borders the eastern boundary of Upper Silesia. Prompted by ideology and greed, the Nazis incorporated these areas into Greater Germany. German settlers had developed Upper Silesia centuries earlier, and the Nazis wished to regain land they saw as theirs. And although Germans had not settled Zaglembie, it was tied economically to Upper Silesia. Both were agriculturally poor, but great underground wealth of minerals, metallic ores, and coal had given rise to prosperous factories and mining concerns.[6]

May 3rd Street, Sosnowiec, Poland, ca. 1930.
(Courtesy of Jeffrey K. Cymbler)

This industrial development shaped the lives of the Jews. While the Nazis pursued a program of "ethnic cleansing" in most of the annexed territory, deporting Jews and Poles out of the Germanized areas and into the General Gouvernement, their wish to preserve industrial production prevented this action in eastern Upper Silesia and Zaglembie. Poles and Jews, including the Jews of Sosnowiec, remained in their homes.[7]

The Sosnowiec train station was one of
the grand terminals at the turn of the
century. It was there that Sala said goodbye to her family on October 28, 1940.
(Courtesy of Jeffrey K. Cymbler)

Jewish policemen in the Sosnowiec
ghetto. *(Courtesy of the Zaglembie
Landsmanschaft Melbourne, Australia)*

The town of Sosnowiec counted some 130,000 inhabitants in 1938, of whom about 29,000 were Jewish. Some were long-time residents: when Sosnowiec was established as a railway stop in 1858, Jews from nearby Czestochowa moved in to develop the area around the station. Others came later, mostly from the more distant city of Kielce, in search of work. Sosnowiec offered employment in its mines, smelting plants, factories, and, in 1883, a chemical plant in the nearby village of Srodula. By the time Sosnowiec became a city in 1902, it had grown to encompass Srodula and other villages, as well as worker settlements that had mushroomed along the rail lines. A commercial center with large industrial interests, Sosnowiec supported three coal mines, three smelting plants, and two spinning operations. Jews participated in the economy of the city. A thriving community, they built a great synagogue in 1905 and within the next decade hosted a full Jewish life with an array of institutions: a Jewish hospital, schools, and professional organizations.[8] Sala Garncarz's father was a rabbi who taught in those schools.

German troops, followed by the Einsatzgruppen, special squads to murder Polish leaders and terrorize the population, occupied Sosnowiec (Germanized to Sosnowitz during the occupation) on September 4, 1939. Einsatzgruppe leader Udo von Woyrsch executed thirteen Jews that day. Initiating their own local campaign to clean up the city, German soldiers ordered Sosnowiec barbers to shave off the beards of all Jews. The main newspaper in nearby Kattowitz claimed a few days later that there were no "Kaftanjuden" left in Sosnowiec. "How clean those elements now appear!" the newspaper crowed. "The long cork-screw sidelocks are gone, and the faces mostly shaved, and the dirty caftans and the filthy black felt hats have disappeared."[9] An irritated Himmler ordered the men to stop. It wasn't the Germans' job to educate Jews about hygiene, and such practices would not solve the Jewish problem.

It was the Germans' job, however, to appoint a Jewish community leader. Within weeks of occupying Poland, the Germans severed the Jews from the body politic and set up a *Judenrat*, or Council of Elders, in every community. These Jewish Councils were typically composed of prominent men designated by the Germans to carry out their orders, and to deal with the myriad problems of a community under duress.[10] Again, Sosnowiec proved an exception, in that there was little continuity between the prewar Jewish elites and the German-appointed Judenrat. In the first days of the occupation, an officer of some German soldiers abusing a group of Jewish men suddenly demanded who among them were leaders of the Jewish community. Silence reigned until Moshe Merin, a recently elected member of the town's Jewish Council, stepped forward. In his postwar memoir, Konrad Charmatz, a survivor from Sosnowiec, remembered Merin as "a short, thin man with mousy eyes who was known as an idler, as a professional gambler, and who was always looking for a loan, which he would never repay."[11] The Germans appointed him Elder of the Jews. The power he thus gained over his co-religionists did not improve his character. As Charmatz had noted, Merin sought easy money, and his position, with its contacts with Germans and control over Jews, provided multiple opportunities to achieve this goal. Forced labor and bribery led the list.[12]

Heinrich Himmler, appointed plenipotentiary in charge of the "consolidation of the German nation," was in charge of "ethnic cleansing" in the annexed territories.[13] At the same time, he had to protect industrial production in eastern Upper Silesia and Zaglembie. He therefore decided to strip Jews in that area of their businesses and bank accounts, but to permit them and their Polish neighbors to remain where they were. To protect the "purity" of the old Reich, Himmler ordered an internal police boundary (roughly along the former German-Polish border) that effectively imprisoned 850,000 Poles and Jews in a 2,000-square-mile area. This region, which centered on Zaglembie and included the former Duchy of Oswiecim in the south and the Blachstadt area in the north, was now called the *Oststreifen*, or Eastern Strip.[14] The Germans used cities in the Oststreifen, especially Sosnowiec and its neighbor Bedzin, as a dumping ground for Jews from areas west of the internal police boundary. These Jews were assigned to the most squalid homes in the poorest quarters. But the Germans did not order the establishment of enclosed ghettos. Not yet. In this, the situation of Jews in the Oststreifen differed markedly from that of Jews in Lodz or Warsaw.

The whole of the Oststreifen functioned as a ghetto inhabited by Poles and Jews. To facilitate their dealings with the nearly 100,000 Jews in the strip, the Germans established a Central Committee of Councils of Elders and appointed Merin as head. The Central encompassed thirty-seven Jewish communities and swelled into an organization of 1,200 employees. One of its main tasks was to provide forced laborers to the Germans.[15]

The use of Jewish forced labor in Germany had burgeoned with the invasion of Poland and the concomitant enlistment of German men in the armed forces. Jews were seconded to do the most difficult, exhausting, and dirtiest jobs in factories, and they received none of the benefits (paid state vacation days, insurance, additional rations, pensions) accorded to "Aryans." Nor, often, did their employers provide them with tools to do the assigned work. Jewish forced laborers became a fixture in ammunition works and on street-paving and snow-removal crews, and cleaning work was also commonly assigned to them. Jews were guarded at the work site: they arrived together under guard, worked in close formation, were not allowed to speak or move about, and left as they came.[16]

Jews in the annexed territories provided a new pool of forced labor. The sole question was, for whom: the Reich in general, or the SS in particular? Power and politics decided in favor of the latter. As Reich Commissioner for the Consolidation of the German Nation, Himmler had great authority in the area, especially over the populations that in the best of all Nazi worlds were to be deported but for the present could not be: the Poles and Jews. Then, too, the man formally in charge of that annexed district, Fritz Bracht, was Himmler's protégé. Bracht dared not refuse Himmler anything, and Himmler needed cash to fill SS coffers. The SS ran many projects dedicated to the establishment of a racially pure state, but they were not entitled to tax monies to fund them. Control over human beings served as a source of income. Inmates in the SS concentration camp empire worked in SS enterprises.[17] Jews in the Oststreifen could be used for forced labor as well.

By autumn 1940, when it had become clear that the "territorial solution" to the "Jewish problem" would not work, Himmler moved to make the best of a bad situation. He appointed (October 15) the forty-one-year-old SS-Oberführer Albrecht Schmelt, who was also police commissioner of Breslau, as Special Representative of the Reichsführer-SS for the Deployment of Foreign Labor in East Upper Silesia. Schmelt was in charge of Jews in the Oststreifen; Poles seconded to forced labor were sent to the Reich. Aiming for a *Judenrein* Reich, the Nazis at this point in the war did not send Jews west of the police boundary, even as forced labor. Some Poles saw this as a grave injustice and, to escape transport west, tried to be counted as Jews.

The new Special Representative created a department that soon became known as the Schmelt Organization. Its headquarters were in Sosnowiec, and Schmelt ordered Merin to conduct a census of all labor-worthy Jews. With the information provided by Merin and his Jewish police, Schmelt built a comprehensive system of exploitation. His monopoly differed from the more patchwork organization of Jewish forced labor in the Reich or in the General Gouvernement. Schmelt had absolute control. At least 75 percent of the Jews in the Oststreifen had no means of subsistence, and all work flowed through Schmelt.[18]

The Jewish Council became an arm of the Schmelt organization. Merin believed that German dependence on Jewish labor would prove decisive in saving Jews' lives. And he had reason to hold that notion. Living conditions for Jews in Zaglembie were far better than in the enclosed ghettos of Lodz, Warsaw, or other Polish cities. And Schmelt clearly aimed to exploit the labor of Jews, not to push them out of the economy. Jews in Germany were used as forced laborers too, but there they comprised a small percentage of any enterprise. A company could do without them if necessary. In Zaglembie, by contrast, Jewish labor was crucial. Thus, when Jews were called up for forced labor service, they reported for duty. Carrot and stick: they thought that this was a way to survive— and they knew that if they did not show up, the Jewish Council would punish their entire family by withdrawing everyone's food ration coupons.[19]

At first, Jews worked in ammunition plants located in Zaglembie cities or army workplaces in the region, which allowed them to live at home. But Schmelt soon came to appreciate the financial potential of his goldmine. He began to send laborers to camps set up near large ammunition plants, or to railway yards at crucial junctions where their job was to enlarge the grounds. An uncompleted stretch of the Breslau-Gleiwitz autobahn—which, with the possibility of a future war with Russia, was considered of vital military importance—emerged as a major source of income for Schmelt.[20]

Schmelt and Merin made a fortune. Schmelt leased Jews for a daily payment of 6 RM (Reichsmark) per skilled worker and 4.5 RM per unskilled laborer. He triaged the money unequally among his own pocket, the organization (for "room and board"), and Merin. Merin did the same, keeping some for himself, turning some over to the Jewish Council, and allotting male forced laborers 0.5 RM a day and less to women. Schmelt demanded that Merin supply him with workers. Merin, in turn, imposed a minimum head tax of 10 RM—a high bar for the many impoverished Jews—on all able-bodied, non-essential personnel; anyone who could not pay was subject to forced labor. If Merin thought someone could pay a heavier tax, he did not hesitate to impose an arbitrary figure. Thus, he accrued vast sums from Jews desperate to remain at home with their families. He pocketed a portion; the remainder supported the Jewish Council's nine departments: welfare, health, food, finance and budget, labor, education, statistics and archives, administration, and legal matters. While Merin profited enormously from Schmelt's organization, he also established a system of social support that included soup kitchens, milk for young children, child care centers for the children of working parents, vocational training for young people, three orphanages, five homes for the elderly, and a hospital in Sosnowiec. Unlike their co-religionists elsewhere in former Poland, Jews in Zaglembie did not sink into the direst poverty; they had clothes, food, and medical care. If conditions were not good on an absolute scale, they were better than elsewhere. And that mattered. It nourished Merin's megalomania that he was a modern-day Moses, a savior of the Jewish people, and it fueled the Zaglembie Jews' hope that they could endure until the Germans lost the war.[21]

Sala Garncarz's family was too poor to afford the 10 RM head tax. Within a fortnight of Schmelt's appointment as Special Representative, Raizel Garncarz, Sala's next older sister, received a summons for forced labor service. The family counted six daughters (three lived with their parents in a one-room apartment, one had died before the war, and two were married) and five sons (one married, one in the Polish army, one who had fled to Russia in 1939, and two who had died before the war). Sala, at sixteen the youngest in the family, volunteered to take the deeply religious and somewhat cantankerous Raizel's place. No one knew—not Sala, Raizel, or their parents—what this would mean. They thought Sala would work for a period of time and return to Sosnowiec. In fact, other than one visit home, Sala was caught in the Schmelt web for the duration of the war. As it happened, in her particular case, this proved her salvation.

Sala reported to the Sosnowiec train station for deportation to the Geppersdorf labor camp. Anxious and overwhelmed, she welcomed the kind attention of a woman fifteen years older than she. "If you could have looked deep into my heart," Sala wrote in her diary (October 28, 1940), "you would have seen how desperate I was; still I tried to keep a smile on my face as best I could, though my eyes were filled with tears. One must go on bravely and courageously, even if the heart is breaking." Ala Gartner, daughter of a prosperous family in Sosnowiec, assured Sala's mother that she would look after the young girl. Ala would go on to become a resistance hero at Auschwitz; she was one of four women hanged for their role in smuggling ammunition from their workplace into the camp to be used by the resistance. But that was four years later. In October 1940, she was Sala's hero. The loving relationship that grew between them cheered and sustained Sala in Geppersdorf.

Geppersdorf was one of the Breslau-Gleiwitz autobahn camps, and the use of Jews as forced labor in this enterprise illuminates how the realities of the war shifted the balance between ideology and practice. Known as "the Roads of the Führer," the autobahn had been announced in 1933 as a symbol of the new Germany. This was not simply a highway system. The autobahn was meant to be one of the greatest architectural creations of world history, akin to the pyramids of Egypt, the Acropolis of Athens, or the Great Wall of China. Hitler himself initiated construction (September 23, 1933) near Frankfurt-am-Main, turning the first spade. Celebrated in propaganda, Hitler moving the earth became a central icon, portraying the energy of the new Nazi government, promising an end to unemployment, and intimating a close relationship with the common people. Each time a section was completed, Hitler participated in an elaborate dedication ceremony modeled upon the triumphal marches of Roman emperors.[22]

Each month, prisoners were given an "Eskart" (meal ticket), issued by the labor camp administration, which they had to show to receive their meals. This is one of many that Sala saved.

Hitler's vision demanded tens of thousands of workers able to manage heavy physical labor. Unemployed Germans were forced to take these jobs. Housed in camps along the new road, they were separated from their families for long periods. Their barracks were hot in summer, cold in winter, and utterly ill-equipped with regard to hygiene. Nor was the work well paid. In bad weather, when the men could not work, they were not paid at all.[23]

As employment levels climbed, German workers left the autobahn camps for better jobs. They could earn higher pay in industry, and enjoy the comfort of life at home. But the autobahn still needed to be built. The Anschluss of Austria netted unemployed Austrians for autobahn work; the annexation of the Sudetenland, Sudeten Germans; and the occupation of Bohemia and Moravia, Czech workers. But it was never enough.

The ideology of the autobahn and its accompanying propaganda had accorded the project great prestige, despite the realities of working conditions. Prisoners and Jews were not considered worthy to work on a venture so closely related to Hitler. Strapped for labor, however, a compromise solution (June 1939) put Jews to work as forced labor in quarries that supplied building materials for the roads. Aryans would work on the road.[24] The wartime manpower shortage shifted the ground once again: prisoners and forced laborers from occupied countries were sent to work on the roads. In May 1940, autobahn crews comprised some 19,000 regular workers and 28,000 forced laborers and prisoners. Half a year later, Schmelt added Jews, sending them to camps vacated by Aryan workers. Geppersdorf was one of these camps, with 350 to 500 Jewish forced laborers (leased by Schmelt to the Moll and Mathies firms) working on the autobahn.[25]

Conditions in the camps did not improve, of course. Men worked for twelve hours a day. Heavy labor and lack of medical care took a high toll: many died and were buried just outside the camp grounds. The workers were not free to leave, nor did they get sick pay or any other benefits. But as they were paid—although only a pittance—this was still forced labor and not the slave labor of Auschwitz and other SS camps. Furthermore, workers were fed real food; they were hungry but they did not starve. Most forced laborers were men, but some camps had a separate section to house women laborers who worked in the kitchen, kept the camp, and served as secretaries, seamstresses, and the like. Sala was a seamstress at Geppersdorf.

As the Schmelt organization archive did not survive the war, many details about his system remain obscure. A convergence of evidence from a variety of sources strongly suggests, however, that Schmelt had no uniform set of rules—indeed, Schmelt workers did not even have a standard uniform. He

A certificate in German indicating time
Sala spent in Geppersdorf, signed by
the Lagerführer (camp boss) and dated
June 9, 1942. In her letters, Ala urged Sala
several times to obtain this certificate.

IV 196

Es wird hiermit bescheinigt, dass
die Jüdin

Sara Garncarz

sich seit dem 28. Oktober 1940 im hiesi-
gen Arbeitslager befindet und als
Schneiderin eingesetzt war. —

Geppersdorf, den 9. VI. 1942.

Ernst
Lagerführer:

operated on an ad hoc basis, focusing on maximum profit for labor rather than on the rapid annihilation of "undesirable elements." He fell on the pragmatic side of an inherent contradiction that troubled Nazi ideology. Nazis dreamed of a utopian, racist, German-controlled Europe. This called for the murder of many categories of people, foremost among them the Jews. Yet this same vision required the labor of the people who were to be murdered. Committed to their racist dream, some Nazis were willing to forego the labor. Others, like Schmelt, were not. Thus, Schmelt's camps were not characterized by starvation or physical torture.[26]

Schmelt simply did not concern himself with the inmates' letter-writing for the same reason. Inmates received and sent letters primarily through two main channels: the regular postal system, and a community mailbag that took letters from inmates to the Jewish community offices, where families gathered to receive news from their loved ones. Raizel urged her sister (December 1, 1940) to use the post. "Probably the best is to write by mail and after 2 days one receives the mail, while it takes 10–12 days through the community." Letters also trickled between inmates at different labor camps, sometimes in the form of postcards and sometimes through the use of a form on which individual inmates in one camp registered their greetings to specific inmates at another camp. Regulations appear to have fluctuated. Inmates were usually permitted to write one postcard every fortnight, and receive mail more often. But Raizel noted in a letter of December 1, 1940, that the family had received six cards to date; i.e., every five to six days (although the flow was never even) rather than fourteen. No matter how many postcards the family received, Raizel, a regular correspondent, constantly bemoaned her younger sister's slack communication. "What should we do if we receive no answer from you," she scolded in a letter of December 16, 1940, "we write 5 times before we get one answer." Or again, on January 6, 1941: "Our ordeals are beyond words. How can you neglect us by not writing to us for such a long time? One would have thought you would try, but no!" Clearly, Sosnowiec Jews (such as Raizel) expected labor camp inmates to be able to correspond with them.

Frequency of exchange was not the only regulation that fluctuated. Initially inmates were permitted to send and receive letters in Polish; by mid-December, however, all communication had to be in German. A postcard from Raizel (January 20, 1941) highlights the consequences of this directive: "Chana

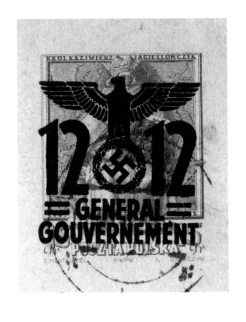

Some of Sala's letters bore stamps from the General Gouvernement (a French designation dating back to World War I), an area in Poland that was not annexed to the Reich. On mail sent from within the Reich, Hindenburg Medallion stamps were most common until 1941, when Adolf Hitler's profile began to appear. Letters were stamped "Z," for *zensiert*, "censored," after inspection. Some camps required that old mail be exchanged for new mail, which would be punched and stored in a large notebook upon arrival.

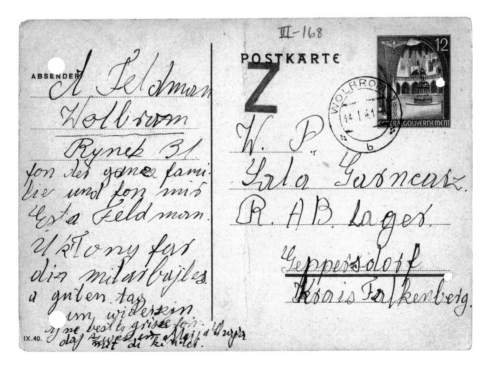

cannot write in German, so I send her regards for her." Inmates were also permitted to receive parcels. In her letters, Raizel carefully noted what they had packed, to ensure that Sala received everything.

Labor pay, mail, and parcels provided physical and social links between Jews at home in Sosnowiec and their friends and relations in camps like Geppersdorf. In response to a query from Sala about money, Raizel lamented (November 24, 1940), "All in all no more than 10 RM for 4 weeks, so you can imagine how we are doing." That figure had not changed by December 1, but a fortnight later she wrote, "Just this week we received 13 Marks." Sala's pay—which went directly to Merin, while she was given some pfennigs of pocket money directly—accounted for a fraction of this sum. The balance came from Jewish communal funds. The Germans had confiscated all Jewish-owned businesses, which were administered by a *Treuhand*, or "trust organization."[27] The Treuhand leased these companies to Germans, who paid a portion of their profits to the trust. A fraction of that sum was paid to Merin, who undoubtedly took much of it for himself. The balance supported an ever more indigent Jewish community. As conditions worsened at home, Sala's income became increasingly important to her family. On May 13, 1941, half a year after her departure, Raizel fumed, "Today we received 4 RM 20 pfennigs, imagine. They say you are entitled to 30 pfennigs per day.... That's what they're saying. Please tell us exactly what you are making, but write clearly." Sala evidently scraped together her pocket money and sent it home as well. These sums came directly from her, and not through the community. "Oh, what a wonderful surprise to receive money from you for the first time!" Raizel exclaimed on July 9, 1941. With "such enormous inflation, the 10 RM come in handy." Acknowledging receipt of 5 RM (August 7, 1941), she emphasized: "they really came in handy this time."

If Sala's pay affected her family's life at home, so did her behavior— or their friends' and relations' perception of it. "The Grünbaum family complains terribly about you, that you treated their son and brother Abram Grünbaum badly," Raizel reported to Sala (January 4, 1941). "The mother fell sick on account of this and she asks why and how he deserves something like this from you." The Grünbaums were cousins. "We ask you to write us about this and to treat him better from now on.... Maybe you could help him as much as you can." She concluded, "I think that this was nothing but a misunderstanding." Abram's sister, Sala's cousin Rozia, wrote to her about this as well: "Sala, one Mrs. Soya from the camp wrote to us that our Abram has trouble with you and that you have not been nice to my brother. How can you do this to him and not act like a cousin." Worried about their loved one, the family begged her "not to forget Abram, because you, Sala, know how it is." Either Mrs. Soya reported incorrectly or the situation changed with time. "Our dear cousin Sala," her relatives effused on May 7, 1941. "Today we received a postcard from our dear child. We all cried with joy because of the good things he said. Dear Sala, how can I express our gratitude for the kindness of your heart as Abram described it to us?"

Friends as well as relations implored Sala to look after their loved ones. Excusing herself for not having written sooner (April 30, 1941)—"I and everybody else always think of you but, unfortunately, we're all going crazy and have no patience to write"—her girlfriend Fela got to the point:

Now, dear Sala, I ask you very much to inquire about Mordtka Weisberg of Sosnowitz, Sudenstrasse 19, now Pokoj 40 at your place. He doesn't write at all. He is and has always been a mentally ill man. And he can't write. Is it possible, maybe, that you could write a card on his behalf every 14 days? You can write to my address. His mother, brothers, and sisters would be forever grateful to you.

The apparent normality of family relations, communal ties, and shared income reflected a precarious stability in the Oststreifen. This was cracked by the German invasion of the Soviet Union in June 1941. Einsatzgruppen followed on the heels of the Wehrmacht, massacring Jewish men, women, and children. First, the army stepped aside, leaving Himmler's men to their work. Active collaboration soon followed, with regular soldiers as well participating in systematic murder. Annihilation became the "final solution" to the "Jewish problem."[28] Once the taboo of killing women and children had been violated in Russia, the Jews of central and western Europe were next on the Germans' list.

By the fall of 1941, Schmelt controlled some 17,000 forced laborers in camps, 8,000 of whom were in sites along the autobahn. The rest worked in camps attached primarily to munitions or chemical plants, or they lived at home.[29] The Schmelt organization established a total of 177 camps, with, for the most part, one to six hundred workers each. The majority were located in Silesia, but some were in the Sudeten German parts of Czechoslovakia. Some 20,000 Jews worked in "shops" (the English word was used) in the Oststreifen, usually textile concerns, sewing uniforms for the Wehrmacht. Children as young as ten went to work in these shops. Men were paid 70 RM a month, women 50. Schmelt took 30 percent for his organization and himself; the balance went to Merin. As with pay for forced labor in the camps, this sum was triaged between Merin's pocket, the Jewish community coffers, and whatever remained to the individual worker.

These jobs provided the backbone of Jewish life in the Oststreifen. Writing to her (May 8, 1941) from one such shop, Sala's friends explained, "We have been working in the shop all this time and we have more work than when you were here and we have had various problems." The issue of employment loomed even larger after the invasion of the Soviet Union. Raizel reported regularly on the family's prospects. September 3, 1941: "Our dear father has work, only Blima doesn't at the moment. Maybe in two weeks. David [brother-in-law] also works in the shop." As time went on, Raizel's worries about this grew. October 21, 1941: "Blima still doesn't have work; it's very difficult to get into the shop, but we reckon she still might; every second is precious." November 8, 1941: "Nothing worked out for Blima. She has to have a [sewing] machine.... Whoever has money gets in, but without money, there's no influence."

Employment was indeed key, but disaster struck in Schmelt's camps before it hit at home. Schmelt's Jewish laborers were a great economic prize, and those who could not work burdened his system. Pioneering the process of selection that would come to characterize the life-or-death entry point at Auschwitz, Schmelt, starting in late fall 1941, sent all Jews in his camps who could no longer work to be murdered in the newly created gas chambers of crematorium I in Auschwitz. They were the first Jews to be killed in that installation. Sala was lucky: she was young and she was healthy. She was not deported to Auschwitz.

Construction on the autobahn stopped in December 1941, but the SS did not close the Schmelt camps connected to that project. These laborers comprised the largest group of Jews under Himmler's control, and he had another job for them. Anticipating victory over the Soviet Union, the Nazis imagined they would rebuild huge tracts of eastern Europe as a Nazi blood-and-soil fantasy, with big farms where veterans would create equally big families. To ensure SS leadership of this plan, Himmler created his own construction empire. On the Reichsführer's instructions, SS chief of construction Hans Kammler drew up a "Provisional Peace Building Program for the Waffen-SS and the German Police," which he presented to his boss in December 1941. Initially budgeted at 13 billion RM, it quickly grew—on paper—to 80 billion. Kammler proposed the organization of roving SS-building brigades composed of prisoners of war, concentration camp inmates, and Jews to actualize the Provisional Peace Program.[30] The Schmelt camps thus began to train Jewish inmates in the building trades, especially concrete construction. At the Wannsee conference (January 20, 1942), which cemented Himmler's control over all Jews in Nazi Europe, Reinhard Heydrich, who chaired the meeting, referred to Kammler's program. "In the course of the Final Solution, the Jews are now to be suitably assigned as labor in the East," he announced. And he continued: "In big labor gangs, with the sexes separated, Jews capable of work will be brought to these areas...."[31]

The Soviet Union was not defeated, of course. And the building brigades never materialized. Schmelt's camp system continued to grow, however, and the inmates were detailed to other work. For young, healthy workers such as Sala, Schmelt's camps proved more secure than life at home in Sosnowiec. In spring 1942, the Jews of the Oststreifen, like their co-religionists in many communities throughout Nazi Europe, fell ever more surely into the lethal maws of what had become the Germans' Final Solution to their Jewish problem: Judeocide; the murder of every Jew.

Like Chaim Rumkowski, the Elder of the Lodz ghetto, and Jacob Gens, the Elder of Vilna ghetto, Merin held on to the idea that the Jews had to make themselves indispensable. He sought to transform his community into an urban work camp. Salvation lay in employment.[32] "[I]t isn't the same as when you were here," Sala's girlfriends explained (March 1, 1942); "we are very burdened and every day brings new torment.... We work from morning until night and we come home very tired, and we want to do nothing. We ask only that we get through the day." Less than three weeks later, some of them had been sent to Schmelt camps. "You will probably be surprised to get mail from me from a camp; my turn, it seems, has come too," her friend Frymka announced (March 19, 1942). "Sala Czarka is with me, we even share a room. I don't have to tell you what it is like here, you already know." Those who remained at home thought their conditions were worse than those in the camps. "We're in such a daze and have no time [to write]," a dispirited Sala Rabinowicz wrote (April 6, 1942).

And our thoughts are foggy, too, we have no energy or patience to write to you. Yours is a quiet life, you have no worries. The days pass quickly with work and you don't have to worry about tomorrow. But we—

I'm working as usual.... Gucia also works from early in the morning until 7 o'clock. Chana tries to get an assignment for her brother from the commission and, I believe, he will go away to work also....

We have nothing but worries.... You live in a different world, there are so many new things going on and we are curious to know about everything.

Sala's friend was correct. As the war against Russia claimed ever greater resources, the Germans redeployed the men along the police boundary that separated the Oststreifen from the rest of Upper Silesia.[33] What had been a de facto enormous 2,000-square-mile ghetto was no longer guarded, and systematic deportations of Jews from the area to Auschwitz ensued.[34]

A transport of 630 from Dabrowa arrived on May 3; some 1,500 Sosnowiec Jews were sent to Auschwitz that same month. Inmates in camps were beside themselves with anxiety about their families at home. "I guess you'll be impatient by now, but what can I do? My head keeps spinning, my head, it's just awful, but Sala, don't worry about us, we're home," Raizel reassured her sister (May 14, 1942). And she continued, "How lucky you are! Be happy, be glad and thank God a thousand times every day that you still have somebody to whom you can write, with the way things are going here." Words failed Raizel. She did not know how to convey the catastrophe. "Sala, remember how lucky you are, you have no idea."

Another 200 Jews were shipped to Auschwitz in June. Smaller transports followed. The Garncarz family were not among the targeted. They remained until the great selection and deportation of Zaglembie Jews began in August 1942. Some 50,000 Jews from Sosnowiec, Bedzin, and Dabrova were ordered to report to the sports stadium. Jewish youth movement leaders urged Jews not to go, to resist deportation. Desperately, they sought to organize underground resistance cells and to make contact with Polish underground movements. All to no avail. Some advocated armed defense; others pressed fellow Jews to flee. Both approaches came to naught.[35]

Gestapo and Schmelt men conducted the selection. About 18,000 people who had papers showing that they were forced laborers returned home that night. More than 30,000 remained in the sports field, without food or water, for three days. Some 9,000 were selected for the Schmelt organization. The rest— the elderly, young, pregnant, and ill—were shipped to Auschwitz. Still Merin believed that his policy of cooperation with Schmelt had saved Jews. "I feel like a captain whose ship was about to sink and who succeeded in bringing it safe to port by casting overboard a great part of his precious cargo," he announced to the Jewish Council.[36]

Sala's sisters Raizel and Blima were selected for Schmelt camps. "I am sure you are wondering where we got this address in Neusalz from, but it's for real," Raizel wrote to Sala (August 21, 1942). "That's what happened. Blima, Sala Cz., Frymke and I are together. Fate has brought us here." She had one bit of good news: their older sister Laya Dina and her husband and children remained in Sosnowiec. Laya Dina confirmed the news in a postcard a week later (August 28). Reassuring notices continued for a time. "Don't worry about your parents, everything is fine," Ala comforted her (September 20). Sala heard from her cousin Rozia in October that she was still in Bedzin, where she worked in a shop. That same month the remaining Jews in Sosnowiec and Bedzin were enclosed in the adjacent suburbs of Srodula and Kamionka, respectively. But heartening postcards from home continued to bring cheer to Sala. "Regards from our dear parents," Laya Dina wrote in December. She'd heard from Blima and Raizel: "They are well and have light work." Laya Dina worked "in a factory from 5 o'clock until 5 at night." Her husband "David works in the city administration." The family no longer received Sala's pay, however. "Regarding the payment from your work through the community I can't get it, so see if you can," Laya Dina advised her a month later (January 21, 1943).

The Germans still needed labor. And Schmelt still wanted to run his camps. When deportations from the ghettos in August 1942 narrowed the supply of Jewish workers, he began to pull men from Auschwitz-bound trains. Some 8,000 to 10,000 Jews from Belgium, France, and the Netherlands thus ended up in Schmelt camps.[37]

This suited the Germans. While whole communities were liquidated and deportation trains steamed at all hours, the Germans used the Schmelt camps as a propaganda tool. When the British made a formal statement in the House of Commons (December 17, 1942) on behalf of eleven allied governments clearly articulating that the Germans "are now carrying into effect Hitler's oft-repeated intention to exterminate the Jewish people of Europe," the Germans responded with a splashy article about a Schmelt camp. "In a Jewish Camp in the East: Encounter with Jews from Paris," by Fritz Fiala in the German-language newspaper *Pariser Zeitung*, carried the subtitle: "A visual lesson to counter Roosevelt's tale of horror." Using the fact that the inmates of this camp were Polish Jews from Zaglembie as well as French deportees, Fiala claimed that what we now know was a unique situation reflected the general condition of Jews in the east. The article included photographs and an interview with Merin, who described the situation in Zaglembie in rosy terms. Fiala also included a statement by an unnamed French Jew who praised the Schmelt system. "I wish the whole world could get to know this German achievement and this German humanity," Fiala quoted the inmate as saying. "If we experience an injustice, it is at most that we are here—even if we do not lack anything, and we are not hungry for a moment—while so many Jews remain in their old environment."[38]

Exploiting Jews made Schmelt rich, and he had no intention of losing his grip on his forced labor corps. The Schmelt Jews continued to be protected from the worst of the Nazi system, especially when a particular camp was out of the way. In this respect, Sala was lucky. She had been sent out of Geppersdorf in July 1942 and transferred in turn to a number of Schmelt camps. Finally, in December 1942, she was shipped to a textile factory in Schatzlar, Czechoslovakia. Established a half year earlier, the camp quartered 120 women who worked in a spinning mill owned by Buhl and Söhne.[39] Separated from Auschwitz by a mountain range, the Jewish inmates at Schatzlar were far removed from the deportations. Their families were not.

Himmler's subordinate Fritz Bracht began a campaign to replace Jewish forced laborers with Poles. Himmler himself, perturbed by the Warsaw ghetto uprising, determined once and for all that the only place for Jews was securely incarcerated in camps. He promptly ordered (May 21, 1943) the deportation of all Jews from the Reich to the east and detailed Eichmann to discuss the liquidation of the Srodula and Kamionka ghetto and the future of the Schmelt camps with Schmelt.[40]

Deportation and liquidation began on June 19. Merin and his staff were taken first. In the next days, 5,000 other Jews were shipped to Auschwitz. The entire ghetto was officially liquidated on August 1. Of the 30,000 Jews deported in this *Aktion*, 24,000 were gassed upon arrival at Auschwitz. Some

3,000 Jews escaped and went into hiding, sheltered by Poles. About 1,000 members of Merin's militia remained to clean up the ghetto, removing corpses from the streets, and collecting belongings. In December they too were sent to Auschwitz.[41]

Schmelt inmate correspondence continued through July. "I'm trying this one last time to write to you, Sala. If you're not going to reply, that's just fine. If it's all right with you that your sisters should have to suffer so much … so be it," Raizel began a postcard (July 6, 1943) from her camp in Neusalz to Sala in Schatzlar. "What happened to your conscience? … Isn't it enough that we have no mail from our dear Laya Dina, no news from our dear parents?" A fortnight later (July 19) she lamented, "I haven't heard a word from Laya Dina for two months."

Her fears were well founded. Laya Dina, David, and their children were deported, as were the parents. And with the liquidation of the Zaglembie ghettos, the Schmelt organization became a shadow of its former self. Schmelt's camps were incorporated into the larger SS camp system. Many became satellites of Auschwitz and Gross Rosen, ruled by those Kommandants. Schmelt got a cushy job in Oppeln. Inter-camp correspondence ceased. Distant from both Gross Rosen and Auschwitz, Schatzlar was not integrated into these concentration camps. Largely forgotten by the Nazis, the 120 Jewish women in Schatzlar, Sala among them, survived.

[1] Little has been written on the Schmelt camps. A useful summary in English is Alfred Konieczny, "The 'Schmelt Organisation' in Silesia," in Marcin Wozinski and Janusz Spyra, eds., *Jews in Silesia* (Krakow: Ksiegarnia Akademicka, 2001), 173–79. Most of the extant literature is either in Polish or German. We found the following particularly useful: Alfred Konieczny, "Die Zwangsarbeit der Juden in Schlesien im Rahmen der 'Organisation Schmelt,'" in Götz Aly, ed., *Sozialpolitik und Judenvernichtung: gibt es eine Ökonomie der Endlösung?*, Beiträge zur nationalsozialistischen Gesundheits- und Sozialpolitik, vol. 5 (Berlin: Rotbuch, 1987), 91–110; and Sybille Steinbacher, *"Musterstadt" Auschwitz: Germanisierungspolitik und Judenmord in Ostoberschlesien* (Munich: K.G. Saur, 2000). A good French study is Charles Baron, "Ces camps dont on a oublie le nom: Les ZAL. Camps de traveaux forces pour Juifs en Haute et Basse Silésie," *Le Monde Juif*, 110 (1983), 58–74; 111 (1983), 85–115. One of the few memoirs by an inmate of the Schmelt camps is Hans-Werner Wollenberg, *... und der Alptraum wurde zum Alltag: Autobiographischer Bericht eines jüdischen Arztes über NS-Zwangsarbeitslager in Schlesien (1942–1945)*, ed. Manfred Brusten (Pfaffenweiler: Centaurus-Verlagsgesellschaft, 1992). Written in 1947, Wollenberg's memoir provides a vivid picture of life in the camps.

[2] For a general history of the Holocaust, see Debórah Dwork and Robert Jan van Pelt, *Holocaust: A History* (New York: W.W. Norton, 2002).

[3] As quoted in Dwork and van Pelt, *Holocaust*, 206.

[4] Debórah Dwork and Robert Jan van Pelt, *Auschwitz: 1270 to the Present* (New York: Norton, 1996), 119f.

[5] Dwork and van Pelt, *Holocaust*, 216ff.

[6] Our information about Zaglembie and the (Jewish) history of Sosnowiec derives from Meir Shimon Geshuri, *Sefer Sosnowiec ve-ha-seviva be-Zaglembie* (Tel Aviv: Sosnowiec Societies in Israel and the United States, France, and other countries, 1973–74); this book is partly translated into English by Lance Ackerfeld and Osnat Ramaty, and made available on the Internet as *The Book of Sosnowiec and the Surrounding Region in Zaglebie* [*sic*] by JewishGen, Inc. and the Yizkor Book Project at www.jewishgen.org/yizkor/Sosnowiec/Sosnowiec.html; see also the chapter "Sosnowiec" in *Pinkas Hakehillot Polin: entsiklopedyah shel ha-yishuvim ha-Yehudiyim le-min hivasdam ve-`ad le-ahar Sho'at Milhemet ha-`olam ha-sheniyah* (Encyclopedia of Jewish Communities, Poland), 7 vols., ed. Danuta Dabrowska and Abraham Wein (Jerusalem: Yad Vashem, 1976–99), 7: 327–38; the entry on Sosnowiec is translated into English by

Lance Ackerfeld, and made available on the Internet by JewishGen, Inc. and the Yizkor Book Project at www.jewishgen.org/yizkor/pinkas_poland/pol7_00327.html.

[7] See Dwork and van Pelt, *Auschwitz: 1270 to the Present*, 163ff.; Steinbacher, *"Musterstadt" Auschwitz*, 92ff., 105ff.

[8] Geshuri, *Sefer Sosnowiec*, 217ff.

[9] As quoted in Steinbacher, *"Musterstadt" Auschwitz*, 57.

[10] See Isaiah Trunk, *Judenrat: The Jewish Councils in Eastern Europe Under Nazi Occupation* (New York: Macmillan, 1972).

[11] Konrad Charmatz, *Nightmares: Memoirs of the Years of Horror Under Nazi Rule in Europe, 1939–1945,* trans. Miriam Dashkin Beckerman (Syracuse: Syracuse University Press, 2003), 14.

[12] On Merin see Philip Friedman, "Two 'Saviors' Who Failed: Moses Merin of Sosnowiec and Jacob Gens of Vilna," *Commentary*, 21 (1958), 479–91; and Philip Friedman, "The Messianic Complex of a Nazi Collaborator in a Ghetto: Moshe Merin of Sosnowiec," in Ada Friedman, ed., *Roads to Extinction: Essays on the Holocaust* (New York and Philadelphia: The Jewish Publication Society, 1980), 353–64.

[13] See Dwork and van Pelt, *Auschwitz*, 127ff.; Robert Lewis Koehl, *RKFDV: German Resettlement and Population Policy, 1939–1945: A History of the Reich Commission for the Strengthening of Germandom* (Cambridge: Harvard University Press, 1957).

[14] See Steinbacher, *"Musterstadt" Auschwitz*, 75ff., 109ff.

[15] Ibid., 121ff.; "Sosnowiec" in *Pinkas Hakehillot Polin*, 7: 333f.

[16] See Konrad Kwiet, "Nach dem Pogrom: Stufen der Ausgrenzung," in Wolfgang Benz, ed., *Die Juden in Deutschland 1933–1945* (Munich: Beck, 1988), 581.

[17] See Dwork and van Pelt, *Auschwitz: 1270 to the Present*, 171ff.

[18] Konieczny, "Die Zwangsarbeit der Juden in Schlesien," 95ff.; Steinbacher, *"Musterstadt" Auschwitz*, 138ff.

[19] Konieczny, "Die Zwangsarbeit der Juden in Schlesien," 101f.

[20] Konieczny, "Die Zwangsarbeit der Juden in Schlesien," 102f.; Steinbacher, *"Musterstadt" Auschwitz*, 145ff.

[21] Konieczny, "Die Zwangsarbeit der Juden in Schlesien," 95ff.; Steinbacher, *"Musterstadt" Auschwitz*, 153ff.; "Sosnowiec" in *Pinkas Hakehillot Polin*, 7: 333ff.

22 Erhard Schütz and Eckhard Gruber, *Mythos Reichsautobahn: Bau und Inszenierung der "Strassen des Führers" 1933–1941* (Berlin: Christoph Links, 1996).

23 Ibid., 66ff.

24 Ibid., 84ff.

25 See Martin Weinmann, ed., *Das nationalsozialistische Lagersystem* (Frankfurt-am-main: Zweitausendeins, 1990), 643.

26 Yet life in these camps was harsh enough. See Wollenberg, *... und der Alptraum wurde zum Alltag*, 56ff.

27 The *Haupttreuhandstelle Ost* (Main Trusteeship Office, East) served as an umbrella administration for all such trust organizations. The Haupttreuhandstelle Ost answered to Heinrich Göring as head of the Four-Year Plan. Its local office, the Treuhand Ost, Kattowitz controlled the property of Zaglembie Jews. All agricultural property was controlled by Heinrich Himmler as plenipotentiary for German settlement in the annexed territories. See Steinbacher, *"Musterstadt" Auschwitz*, 86ff.

28 See Dwork and van Pelt, *Holocaust*, 259ff.

29 Konieczny, "Die Zwangsarbeit der Juden in Schlesien," 102ff.; Steinbacher, *"Musterstadt" Auschwitz*, 149.

30 See Dwork and van Pelt, *Auschwitz: 1270 to the Present*, 296ff.

31 Quoted in Lucy Dawidowicz, ed., *A Holocaust Reader* (New York: Behrman House, 1976), 78.

32 For a general discussion of the "Rescue-Through-Work" strategy and Merin's use of it see Trunk, *Judenrat*, 400ff.

33 Steinbacher, *"Musterstadt" Auschwitz*, 285f.

34 "Sosnowiec" in *Pinkas Hakehillot Polin*, 7: 335.

35 Ibid., 335ff.

36 Friedman, "Two 'Saviors' Who Failed," 483.

37 A description of the selection procedure in Cosel can be found in Wollenberg, *... und der Alptraum wurde zum Alltag*, 56f. According to the Kommandant of Auschwitz, Rudolf Höss, Schmelt's men not only pulled healthy men from the trains, they also used those transports to send disabled workers, and even corpses, to Auschwitz. "This created serious difficulties such as delayed trains running late," Höss recalled in his postwar memoirs written in a Polish jail. "This continued until my complaints finally moved the higher SS and Police leaders to put an end to it." Rudolf Höss, *Death Dealer: The Memoirs of the SS Kommandant at Auschwitz*, ed. Steven Paskuly, trans. Andrew Pollinger (Buffalo: Prometheus, 1992), 230.

[38] Fritz Fiala, "In einem Judenlager im Osten. Begegnungen mit Juden aus Paris. Anschauungsunterricht gegen Roosevelts Greuelmärchen," *Pariser Zeitung*, December 20, 1942; as quoted in Steinbacher, *"Musterstadt" Auschwitz*, 156f. Fiala was an editor-in-chief of the *Grenzbote*, and had some experience in writing upbeat stories about concentration camps. In the summer of 1942 he visited Auschwitz to write about the happy fate of Slovak Jews sent to that camp. This article became an important piece of evidence in the Eichmann trial.

[39] Weinmann, ed., *Das national-sozialistische Lagersystem*, 614.

[40] Steinbacher, *"Musterstadt" Auschwitz*, 296f.

[41] "Sosnowiec" in *Pinkas Hakehillot Polin*, 7: 336f.

The Curator's Sala

Jill Vexler, Guest Curator

There is an art to curating an exhibition: distilling the most important information and selecting objects with which to tell the story, imbuing the texts with warmth and clear narrative, and designing an appropriate and welcoming setting. It is a choreography of object, word, and interpretation. The curator's response to the material directly influences what visitors will see, and maybe feel. As a curator, I constantly visualize ways to transform the story and objects into an exhibition—a tangible, visible, aesthetic environment.

A year and a half of reading Sala's letters has taken me into the world of Nazi labor camps, Sosnowiec ghetto life, the Nazi war machine, and, most of all, the Garncarz family. The sheer fact that Sala's medium is letters and postcards resonates deeply with me: I have written and saved letters since I was ten and still have my first fountain pen. And I am convinced that the only way to begin to understand the Holocaust is to listen to the stories of individuals.

The NYPL exhibition came with certain givens. It would be chronological because we were presenting a young woman's movements from 1940 to 1946. Texts had to set the stage in the labor camps, not the death camps with which people are more familiar. It had to highlight Sala's three principal correspondents: her sister Raizel, her mentor Ala Gertner, and Harry, her camp boyfriend. Selection from the 300 letters was simplified by certain essentials. The first item in the exhibition would be Sala's diary, so eloquent that I still cry each time I read it. The last would be the first letter Sala wrote after liberation, to her two surviving sisters. The letters in between, which walk visitors through Sala's five years, were chosen after repeated reading and countless conversations with Sala's daughter, Ann.

Seeing an exhibition is a physical experience, as the voice of the curator escorts visitors through visual information, different from but complementary to the experience of reading a book. Each tells us about a young woman who, throughout five years of fear, horror, and loneliness, never lost herself in a morass of anger and bitterness. I care about Sala and what happened to her. From her, we learn about communicating, loving, giving hope, and rebuilding after disaster.

Suggested Reading

Bauer, Yehuda, with the assistance of Nili Keren. *A History of the Holocaust*. Revised edition. New York: Franklin Watts, 2001.

Dawidowicz, Lucy. *A Holocaust Reader*. New York: Behrman House, 1976.

Dobroszycki, Lucjan, and Barbara Kirshenblatt-Gimblett. *Image Before My Eyes: A Photographic History of Jewish Life in Poland, 1864–1939*. New York: Schocken Books, 1977.

Dwork, Debórah, and Robert Jan van Pelt. *Auschwitz: 1270 to the Present*. New York: Norton, 1996.

Dwork, Debórah, and Robert Jan van Pelt. *Holocaust: A History*. New York: W.W. Norton, 2002.

Fremont, Helen. *After Long Silence: A Memoir*. New York: Delacorte Press, 1999.

From a Ruined Garden: The Memorial Books of Polish Jewry. Edited and translated by Jack Kugelmass and Jonathan Boyarin; with geographical index and bibliography by Zachary M. Baker. 2nd, expanded edition. Bloomington: Indiana University Press, 1998.

Gilbert, Martin. *The Routledge Atlas of the Holocaust*. 3rd edition. London and New York: Routledge, Taylor & Francis Group, 2002.

The Holocaust and Other Genocides: History, Representation, Ethics. Edited by Helmut Walser Smith. Nashville, Tenn.: Vanderbilt University Press, 2002.

The Jews of Poland Between Two World Wars. Edited by Yisrael Gutman et al. Hanover: Published for Brandeis University Press by University Press of New England, 1989.

Levi, Primo. *Survival in Auschwitz*. Translated by Stuart Woolf. With a new Afterword: "A Conversation with Primo Levi by Philip Roth." New York: Touchstone, 1995.

Richmond, Theo. *Konin: A Quest*. London: Jonathan Cape, 1995.

Wiesel, Elie. *Night*. Translated by Marion Wiesel. New York: Hill and Wang, 2006.

Acknowledgments

The history of *Letters to Sala* began in 1991. Since then, I have been helped by a hardy band of friends and family. *Letters to Sala* is the result of our long collaboration.

I am grateful to the survivors who shared their memories: Sala Poznanski, Zusi Ginter, Itka Ginter, Tyla Beeri, Rose Meth, Mala Weinstein, Frymka Zavontz, Sarah Helfand, Gucia Gutman, Dasha Rittenberg, Edith Hendel, and Hokilo Dattner. Ernest Nives, my dear friend, has taught me a thing or two about courage, perseverance, and generosity. I am grateful for the support of the Nives family and the French Children of the Holocaust Foundation, Marina Andrews and the Claims Conference, and Rachel Levin and the Righteous Persons Foundation.

I offer my deep appreciation to an institution I revere, The New York Public Library, and to its president, Paul LeClerc. The exhibition and book were created by Susan Rabbiner, Jeanne Bornstein, Meg Maher, Karen Van Westering, Barbara Bergeron, Kara Van Woerden, guest curator and comrade Jill Vexler, and so many other dedicated people behind the lions. It was my lucky day when David Ferriero came to New York and embraced this project with warmth and wisdom.

Great translators were needed, and luckily I found them: my thanks to Renata Stein for unraveling the difficult German/Yiddish mysteries of the letters. My partnership with Regina Gelb went beyond Polish translation; she has been my teacher and counselor.

To the historians and archivists who shared their expertise, my appreciation for helping a rookie: Zachary Baker, Yehuda Bauer, Volker Berghahn, Jeffrey Cymbler, Debórah Dwork, Israel Gutman, Bella Gutterman, Joke Kniesmeyer, Alfred Koneiczny, Abraham J. Kremer, Avihu Ronen, Mark Rosenthal, and Robert Jan van Pelt.

Without Jane Stine, Lorraine Shanley, and Flip Brophy, I would still be talking instead of writing. To the Sala Advisory Council, warm appreciation for your ideas, your support, and your friendship: Maria DiBattista, Elizabeth Dickey, Shelley Fischl, Judith Ginsberg, Geoffrey Hartman, Nancy Hechinger, Richard Hofstetter, Verlyn Klinkenborg, Sara Levinson, Murray Nossel, Lawrence Sacharow, Kate Stimpson, Al Tapper, and Jessica Weber.

I had the good luck and good taste at seventeen to fall in love with Harold Weinberg, who is first among readers and husbands. To him, and to our children, Elisabeth, Caroline, and Peter, I owe a debt of time and attention that I have no doubt they intend to collect. Be kind to the woman who took you to four Super Bowls.

As this long list demonstrates, *Letters to Sala* has many mothers and fathers. I had only one pair, Sala and Sidney Kirschner. Although now your circle of admirers may widen, your children, grandchildren, and great-grandchildren insist that we love and honor you best of all.